WOMEN AND HORSES

WOMEN & HORSES

GILLIAN NEWSUM

Foreword by
Pat Koechlin–Smythe

° THE °
SPORTSMAN'S
PRESS
LONDON

Published by The Sportsman's Press, 1988

© Gillian Newsum 1988

British Library Cataloguing in Publication Data

Newsum, Gillian
    Women and horses.
    1. Livestock. Horses. Riding by women.
    History
    I. Title
    798.2'3'088042

    ISBN 0-948253-29-0

    Photoset and printed in Great Britain by
BAS Printers Limited, Over Wallop, Hampshire

CONTENTS

ACKNOWLEDGEMENTS

Many people have contributed to this book either with practical assistance, or information or encouragement, but I would like particularly to thank the following: Emma Milne, Judith Draper, J.N.P. Watson, Pat Koechlin-Smythe, Dorothy Laird, Liz Edgar, Michael Williams, Penny Hill, Tinka Taylor, Liz Dudden, Mary Holmes, Dawn Wofford, Benet Hennessey, Edward Horswell, Amanda Kavanagh, David Fuller, Dede Marks, Diana Mason, Lorna Johnstone, the late Anthony Crossley, Jennie Loriston-Clarke, Val Long, Cynthia Haydon, Kim Tinkler, Annette Yarrow, Mary Gordon Watson, Jane Holderness-Roddam, Pamela Carruthers, Jo Dawes, Michele Mills, the staff of *Country Life* and *Horse and Hound*, and my husband Jeremy.

The illustration on page 25 and the colour plate of *Queen Victoria on Horseback, 1838* are reproduced by gracious permission of Her Majesty the Queen. I would also like to thank the following for permission to reproduce illustrations in the book:

Aerofilms: p 13
Maymes Ansell: p 65
Alfred Munnings Art Museum: colour plates of *Mrs J. Burden of Syosset, Long Island* (transparency by courtesy of Frost & Reed) and *A Summer Hack on Exmoor* (transparency by courtesy of Richard Green)
Archive Max E. Amman: p 52
Archive Staub: p 43 (top)
Arthur Ackermann & Son: *A Hunting Incident* (colour plate); pp 26, 31 (bottom)
BBC Hulton Picture Library: pp 21, 35, 128 (bottom)
The British Library: p 17 (bottom)
Country Life: pp 40, 43 (bottom), 48 (top)
Gerry Cranham: Gee Armytage riding Gee A and The Princess Royal with Ten No Trumps (colour plates)

John Elliot: pp 85, 105, 147
Frost & Reed: *An Elegant Equestrienne on a Grey* (colour plate)
Giraudon: *Queen Catherine of Westphalia* (colour plate)
Richard Green Gallery: *An Elegant Lady Riding in a park with her spaniel, The Riding School*, and *Emma Anne Mortimer riding her favourite hunter on the seashore* (colour plates)
Peter Harding: pp 73, 77, 90
Hermes Museum, Paris: p 22
Kit Houghton: Melanie Smith on Calypso, the American team at the 1987 Hickstead Nations Cup, Liz Edgar on Everest Forever, Gillian Greenwood, Princess Anne on Saint John, Karen Stives riding Ben Arthur, Lucinda Green and Mins Lincoln, Anne Grethe Jensen and Margit Otto Crepin (colour plates); pp 45, 63, 68, 87, 88, 91, 93–95, 101, 102, 104 (top), 145
Stanley Hurwitz: p 142
Illustrated London News: pp 36, 38
Leslie Lane: Debbie Johnsey riding Moxy (colour plate); 58, 59 (bottom, left), 61, 62, 79 (top), 104 (bottom), 137
The Mansell Collection: pp 15, 27
Jim Meads: pp 119–121
The National Gallery of Scotland: *The Countess of Mar in 1715* (colour plate)
Press Association: p 115
Private Collection: p 30
Punch Publications: *What London Crushes are coming to*, a *Punch* cartoon of 1873 (endpaper)
W.W. Rouch: p 113
Alec Russell: pp 125, 130, 132, 133
The Sladmore Gallery: pp 12, 41, 59 (bottom right)
Sotheby's: p 31 (top)
Sport & General: p 86
York City Art Gallery: p 108
York Racing Museum: p 109

FOREWORD BY
PAT KOECHLIN-SMYTHE OBE

This excellent book gives women riders true recognition of their exploits through the ages with the record of their success in the many facets of equestrian sport. Often, a special empathy that a woman has with animals and especially with a horse, will bring out the best in the partnership.

The quotation from Kipling when he wrote on the she bear 'The female of the species is more deadly than the male', can apply in competition when rider and horse combine concentration and ability, rather than force, to gain top results and deadly accuracy when winning! It has been proved that certain horses will perform well only with a woman rider, because they need to have confidence in the understanding and knowledge that a woman can impart.

It was only after the war in the 1940s that women began to get the attention of the public in equestrian sport. Girls had been successfully keeping the farms and working with horses, while the men were away. The pony clubs were run by busy mothers, whose children had little entertainment or travel. It was usually the girls who took over the ponies and their care, while the boys had other interests.

When I first joined the British team to go abroad in 1947, I was looking after my own horses. By the time I had a girl to help me, she was often the only girl groom at international shows on the continent. Nowadays, girl grooms must be in the majority and special facilities are made available for them. Even racing stables are following this trend too.

The stable care, behind the scenes, is the basis for a horse's well-being and success. A girl groom often has this caring and understanding way for each individual animal. If one of their charges is unwell, they will nurse it, as a mother with a sick child. Some horses too, brilliant with a lady rider, just will not perform with a man. I had two of these, the mare Finality, my first international jumper, and the superb athletic jumper Prince Hal – an ex race horse.

The history of horsewomen through the ages, from the Amazons to present day equestrian sport, makes fascinating reading. The name for a ladies show jumping competition is still the 'Amazons' Prize' on the continent! I am sure that this book will give interest and pleasure to many people.

Pat Koechlin-Smythe

CHAPTER ONE
WARRIORS AND HUNTRESSES

The modern woman has the opportunity to enjoy the full range of activities in the diverse world of horses. She can ride and compete at all levels, or make her career in training, breeding or caring for horses. During the last forty years women have, increasingly, taken advantage of the enormous growth in equestrian sports and related interests, so that in many fields they are now the dominant force. On numerous occasions, though, they have had to break down strong barriers of prejudice and tradition to follow in their chosen pursuits. Only thirteen years ago women in Britain were still barred from National Hunt racing, and it was not until 1978 that they were allowed to compete in high-goal polo.

Today, woman's association with the horse is greater than it has ever been. Because the skill of creating a good partnership with a horse, based on mutual trust and understanding, is as important as the physical demands of riding, women have found that they are able to compete on equal terms with men. The special bond between a man and his horse that was once so vital in the battlefield has now become the female's most valuable weapon in her ability to partake successfully at the highest levels in all equestrian sports.

The link between women and horses in the past was often a tenuous one, based largely on the horse's assistance in the progress of mankind in general. For thousands of years the horse was used and exploited by humans to further their own development – in agriculture and transport, and in war – and without it many of our physical and cultural advances are unlikely to have been achieved. Women's direct association with the horse in those early years was limited mostly to its domestic use, an aspect that received little attention from historians whose main concerns were with the events brought about by war and politics. Since few women rode in battle, their involvement with the horse is not well documented, as only those who had a direct influence on the fortunes of nations merited much space in the history books.

Myth and legend reveal more. Most complete among horsewomen were the Amazons, a nation of women originally from the Caucasus who settled in Cappadocia on the banks of the river Thermodon, by the Black Sea. The correct meaning of the word Amazon is uncertain; literally a-mazos would mean 'no breast', and it is said that they removed their right breast in order to draw their bows more easily. However, there are no con-temporary illustrations to prove these mutilations occurred. The prefix 'a' may even be exaggerative in that the Amazons' great goddess was Artemis of Ephesus, a fertility goddess

Amazon Warrior, a bronze
by Franz von Stuk

who was depicted in a robe that exposed her multiple breasts. The Amazons farmed and hunted and were renowned as riders and breeders of horses, but principally they were warriors. Credited with being the first to employ cavalry, they made numerous excursions into Greece, and founded many towns, including Ephesus, Cyme and Smyrna, and they penetrated Boeotia and Attica. No men were admitted to their society, but once a year the Amazons would 'visit' their neighbours, the Gargarensians. The resultant male children would be returned to their fathers or sacrificed, and only the girls were kept with their mothers.

The Amazons rode astride, for, as warriors, they would have been too insecure and ineffective if they had sat sideways without a saddle. They carried bows, spears or axes, and were usually shown wearing a thin dress, girded at the waist. Their invasion of Attica (the peninsula including Athens) was in revenge for the abduction of Antiope, the sister of the Amazonian queen Hippolyte; when Hercules was set the task of obtaining Hippolyte's girdle as one of his great labours for Eurystheus he had slaughtered the queen and many of her followers, and his friend, Theseus, had carried off Antiope. In the Trojan War, when the Amazons fought on the side of Troy, they lost another queen, Penthesileia, who was killed by Achilles. The notorious beauty, Helen, wife of Menelaus of Sparta, is associated with the huge wooden horse that was used by the Greeks to enter the city of Troy and rescue her.

In Celtic mythology there was a horse goddess, Epona. The White Horse at Uffington

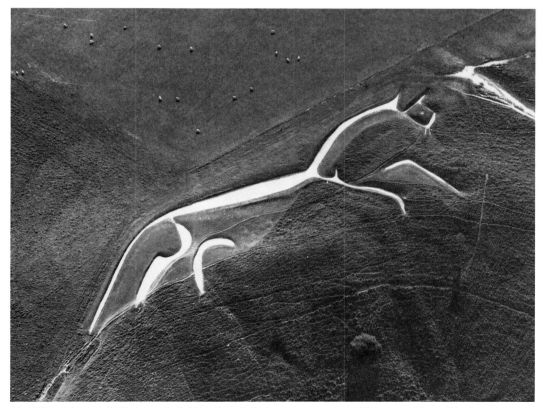

The White Horse at Uffington, Berkshire, thought to be representation of Epona, goddess of the horse. It is 400ft long.

in Berkshire is almost certainly a representation of Epona in zoomorphic form; the horse is about 400ft in total length and has existed, cut into the chalk hill, since the first century BC. Epona, who was sometimes depicted seated sideways on a horse, was unusual for a Celtic god in that she was worshipped over a wide area, stretching from northern Italy, to Spain and to Britain. This seems to have occurred because she was adopted by the much-travelled Roman cavalry as protector of their horses. Generally the class structure of Celtic society restricted worship of gods to the aristocracy, and Epona was fortunate to have been exported around Europe. Similar horse goddesses existed in Ireland and Wales.

Mythology, though not part of our true history, existed in parallel with real events and was, no doubt, very real to people who frequently committed appalling acts and sacrifices as a result of their beliefs. We can, however, be certain of the existence of Boadicea, whose activities in AD 61 were no less bloodthirsty; she is always closely associated with her chariot, drawn by horses.

By 2,000 BC, fortification techniques were well established, but it is doubtful whether armies were mobile. There were carts, but these had four wheels and were pulled by asses or oxen. Horses were to revolutionise warfare in the next four hundred years and remain central to it for at least 3,000 years. The chariot, which came before the cavalry, was a two-wheeled cart drawn by horses with a crew of two (one driving, one fighting). At first they were wooden-wheeled, but with the coming of the Iron Age (roughly 1,000 BC) their robustness would have improved. Chariot driving became quite an art, and Boadicea was probably as adept as any male in controlling her horses. The way in which the British used their chariots in the battlefield was described by Caesar on his second expedition to Britain.

'In chariot-fighting the Britons begin by driving all over the field hurling javelins, and generally the terror inspired by the horses and the noise of the wheels are sufficient to throw their opponents' ranks into disorder. Then, after making their way between squadrons of their own cavalry, they jump down from the chariots and engage on foot. In the meantime their charioteers retire a short distance from the battle and place the chariots in such a position that their masters, if hard pressed by numbers, have an easy means of retreat to their own lines. Thus they combine the mobility of cavalry with the staying-power of infantry; and by daily training and practice they attain such proficiency that even on a steep incline they are able to control the horses at full gallop, and to check and turn them in a moment. They can run along the chariot pole, stand on the yoke, and get back into the chariot as quick as lightning.'

Boadicea was the widow of the King of the Iceni, a powerful tribe in East Anglia which had, nevertheless, been submissive since the Roman invasion. In an apparent political move, the king had appointed the Emperor Nero, who had succeeded Claudius, as joint heir with his two daughters. But the Romans took advantage of his death, plundering the kingdom and humiliating his family. Boadicea's tribe 'was moved to frenzy against the Roman

'Far in the East Boadicea, standing loftily charioted.' (Tennyson.) A painting of Boadicea's attack on Camulodonum by Harvey Payne.

invaders. They flew to arms. Boadicea found herself at the head of a numerous army, and nearly all the Britons within reach rallied to her standard.'[1]

The resultant carnage is unpleasant to contemplate. She moved through Camulodonum (Colchester) towards London, destroying everything and everybody, while the major part of the Roman army was tied up in Anglesey. A similar slaughter occurred in London before she turned back toward the advancing Romans, destroying Verulamium (St Albans) on the way. By now, up to 70,000 people had died at her hands and it was not surprising that the subsequent battle with the Romans should be one with no quarter spared. The professional Roman legions, numbering around 10,000, were pitched against Boadicea's army of 80,000, including their families, and duly won the bloody battle. Boadicea committed suicide.

On a lighter note, and as a digression from warriors, there is the legend of Lady Godiva. She was the wife of the Earl of Mercia, Lord of Coventry, and they were both benefactors of the early church. The Earl made impositions on his tenants with which Godiva disagreed and tried to have removed. Her husband, perhaps in jest, said he would do so only if she would ride naked through Coventry, which she duly did. Her exposure was not in vain, for the Earl kept his side of the bargain. It is a story which lends itself well to embellishment, and there have been various adaptations since it was first recorded in 1236, more than 200 years after the event is supposed to have happened. One version claims that, so as not to embarrass their benefactoress, the worthy people of Coventry all remained indoors with their eyes averted as she rode by, but for one man, a tailor, who peeped through his window and was promptly struck blind.

A saviour on a far greater scale, at least as far as the French are concerned, was the 'Angel of Deliverance', Joan of Arc, who led the French armies to victory over the English at Orleans, opening the way for the coronation of Charles VII at Rheims in 1429. Joan, a peasant maid from the remote hamlet of Domremy on the edge of the Vosge Forest, was commanded by the 'voices' of St Michael, St Margaret and St Catherine to lead the armies of liberation. She made the perilous journey across France to find the King and tell him of her mission. 'I am Joan the Maid, sent on the part of God to aid you and the kingdom, and by His order I announce that you will be crowned in the city of Rheims.' She restored the spirits of the ailing troops and became an inspiration to even the roughest soldier. She won twenty encounters with the British, receiving a number of wounds, but in May 1430 was taken prisoner outside the gates of Compiègne. A year later she was condemned as a heretic by the English-dominated church in Rouen and burnt at the stake. History records the comment of an English soldier who witnessed the scene: 'We are lost. We have burnt a saint.' She was formally canonised in 1920 by Pope Benedict XV.

In fifteenth-century Europe, when Joan of Arc led her troops to battle, the soldiers were mounted on 'Great Horses', huge animals especially developed to strengthen the effect of charging cavalry. Dressed in full armour and carrying a lance, Joan of Arc rode astride on a saddle with high pommel and cantle to hold her firmly in position. Some fifty years

Elaborately dressed for riding, with wig and satin shoes; *The Countess of Mar in 1715* by Godfrey Kneller.

Queen Catherine of Westphalia, wife of Jerome Bonaparte, by Antoine Jean Gros.

Girl riding pillion. A fifteenth-century woodcut of May Day from a Flemish Calendar of Shepherds.

The Wife of Bath from Chaucer's *Canterbury Tales*. She is depicted riding astride, whereas the Prioress and Nun were illustrated riding sideways.

17

earlier the notion of riding side saddle had been introduced to Britain by Richard II's wife, Anne of Bohemia. Until then, women had usually ridden astride in a split skirt, or pillion behind a man. The adoption of a sideways position, whereupon women sat on a stuffed seat resting their feet on a wooden platform known as a planchette, was certainly more elegant but it gave the rider very little control over her horse. It was suitable for journeys at a slow pace, or for more formal occasions attended by ladies of high birth, but any woman who wanted to enjoy the pleasures of riding at greater speeds, particularly in the hunting field, would not have thanked Anne of Bohemia for introducing such an impracticable fashion.

The adoption of the side saddle was not universal. It is clear from illustrations of the Middle Ages that some women still rode astride. In the Ellesmere manuscript of *The Canterbury Tales*, the Prioress and Nun are depicted riding sideways, whereas the Wife of Bath rides astride, and some sixteenth-century French tapestries show women riding both sideways and astride. As late as the eighteenth century – long after the side saddle was in general use – Catherine II of Russia preferred the 'cross saddle' and insisted that all the ladies of her court follow suit, while in the court of Louis XV, it is said that those women who wanted to hunt were obliged to take lessons at the Versailles manège, where they rode astride in high boots and long, divided skirts.

★   ★   ★

I pass many hours on horseback, and, I'll assure you, ride stag-hunting, which I know you'll stare to hear of. I have arrived to vast courage and skill in that way, and am as well pleased with it as with the acquisition of a new sense.

Lady Mary Wortley Montagu (1689–1762): Letter to the Countess of Mar

Fashion and social etiquette largely dictated how and when women rode horses. Their presence in the hunting field, for example, was not always accepted: at the beginning of the nineteenth century in Britain hunting was regarded as neither safe nor respectable for women. However, the women of fifteenth and sixteenth century Europe, swept up in the Renaissance ideal of the complete man and woman for which riding and hunting were regarded as a school for life and character, were generally welcomed in the hunting field, and many were renowned for their expertise and bravery.

Europe's Renaissance period is remarkable for its high proportion of female rulers, many of whom showed outstanding ability in their roles, and who were also keen huntresses. Women of the court during this period were particularly well educated, in languages, art, music and literature, and also in hunting, for it was a time when knowledge of venery was a socially desirable attribute; hunting was not merely a sport, but an art and a science, and experts on the subject were revered.

One woman in particular who took this form of education very seriously was Anne de Beaujeu (1460–1522), daughter of Louis XI, who established an *école de moeurs* for young ladies of high birth, and in later years wrote a book of *enseignements*, explaining her methods and ideas on education. But first and foremost she was a huntress. According to Lady Apsley (*Bridleways Through History*), Anne de Beaujeu 'hunted as she lived – thoroughly, without heeding time, discomfort, fatigue or anything but the hunt on hand.' She had as much knowledge as a professional huntsman, and was responsible for providing the foundation stock of the famous Royal White Hounds of France. As Regent to her younger brother (later Charles VIII), she was said to be energetic, obstinate, cunning and unscrupulous. Her final ambition, the acquisition of Brittany, was achieved in 1490, after she had the audacity to conduct a hunt right into that territory. She arranged for Charles to marry the fifteen-year-old Anne of Brittany, thus securing the land for France.

A sixteenth-century lady. From *Horses in Shakespeare's England* by Anthony Dent.

Among Anne de Beaujeu's pupils at her court was Margaret of Austria, daughter of Maximilian I. Before Anne's conquest of Brittany, Margaret had been betrothed to the young dauphin, and had been sent to France to be educated. Her mother, Mary of Burgundy, is thought to have been the originator of the forward-facing side saddle position, as she rode with her leg wrapped round the pommel of a man's saddle. In the French court, under the influence of Anne de Beaujeu, Margaret excelled at music, painting and embroidery, and enjoyed hunting, but after eight years she was sent home because Anne, ruthless to the end, had decided that it was more important for her brother to marry the heiress of Brittany.

Margaret's subsequent marriages both ended tragically. Her first, to the eighteen-year-old Don Juan, heir to the throne of Spain, lasted only five months before her young husband was dead, and the daughter that Margaret was expecting at that time died soon after birth. Returning to the Netherlands, Margaret married Philibert, Duke of Savoy, but after three years was widowed once more. She was only twenty-six when her second husband died, but she did not remarry. Her time was soon fully occupied in the role of Regent to her young nephew, Charles, who had inherited the vast Hapsburg territory that included all of Spain, Burgundy and the Holy Roman Empire. The House of Hapsburg had few friends left in Europe at this time, but Margaret successfully ruled the inheritance for eight years as well as being Regent of the Netherlands, a job which she retained at the request of her nephew when he came of age.

Margaret's love of hunting manifested itself in the commissioning of the famous *Belles Chasses* tapestries, twelve large panels portraying hunting scenes, designed by Bernard van Orlay; these now hang in the Louvre. She shared her enthusiasm for the sport with her first mother-in-law, Queen Isabella of Spain, one of the greatest of the Renaissance rulers. Isabella succeeded to the throne of Castile soon after marrying Ferdinand of Aragon, and subsequently embarked on a long and arduous series of campaigns to bring about the unification of Spain. According to Lady Apsley, 'she was constantly riding from one end of Castile to the other, making speeches, attending conferences, sitting up all night dictating to her secretaries, holding court all morning, riding a hundred miles or two over mountain passes to plead with some lukewarm supporter for 500 soldiers.'

A deeply religious, energetic and patriotic woman, Isabella helped to develop Spain into a powerful nation, encouraging art, music and literature, and even gave financial support to Christopher Columbus for his sea voyages. One of her greatest passions was the horse. She established stud farms in Andalusia and other parts of Spain that became famous throughout Europe at a time when horse breeding was one of the most valuable industries in the world. She was always well mounted, and on State occasions she and her horse would be lavishly attired. On her way to Mass she 'sat beautifully on her white horse with its gilded saddle and caprisons of gold and silver, wearing a silk shirt woven with pearls, surrounded by her grandees, soldiers and musicians'.

Four years before Isabella's death in 1504 one of the greatest huntresses of the Renaissance was born. Her name was Diane de Poitiers, and she takes her place among the most beautiful women in history. She too was educated in the 'school' of Anne de Beaujeu following her marriage at an early age to the most renowned veneur in France, Louis de Breze, Grand Seneschal of Normandy, son of the Regent's keeper of hounds. With her husband

Diane de Poitiers, acknowledged as the greatest expert on hunting in the court of Francis I of France. In this painting she is represented as the Goddess Diana.

21

and Anne de Beaujeu as guides it is easy to see why Diane ultimately became acknowledged as the greatest expert on hunting at the Court of Henri II.

'No lady was ever better on horseback,' wrote the French historian Brantôme. 'She was very lovely of face and figure.' Her charms soon won the heart of the young Duc d'Orleans, the future Henri II, despite being seventeen years his senior, and she retained her considerable influence over him even after his marriage to the Italian Catherine de Medici. Diane's husband had died when she was just over thirty – an age at which most

Lavishly decorated saddle of the seventeenth century. The rider faced sideways to the horse and rested her feet on the wooden board (or planchette).

of the ladies who adorned the Court of Francis I would have been considered a little long in the tooth – but Diane had a strong constitution and the willpower to ensure that she kept her looks and figure. According to Jehanne d'Orliac, she subjected herself to rigorous discipline, 'rising at three in the morning, she went for a three hours' ride, then had a bath and went back to bed, meditated in solitude and relaxation, ate sparingly and gave the rest of her day to society.' Her liasion with Henri II caused its share of malicious gossip, but Diane remained one of the most prominent women of his court, hunting until she was well over fifty. Henri II created her Duchesse de Valentinois, giving her valuable lands and castles, including the ancient Royal Palace of Chenonceaux, where she created some of the finest gardens of Renaissance France.

According to Charles Chevenix Trench in *A History on Horsemanship*, Diane went hunting 'cross saddle', which may have accounted for her prowess in the hunting field. It was customary for the ladies of the Court of Francis I and Henri II to sit sideways, giving them far less control of the horse than they would have had astride, and they must have felt extremely insecure at anything more than a gentle trot. When Henri II's wife, Catherine de Medici, took to the hunting field (perhaps to win the favour of her husband who was still infatuated with Diane de Poitiers) she had numerous falls, once breaking her leg and another time fracturing her skull. As Mary of Burgundy is thought to have done, Catherine tried riding in a forward-facing position with one leg hooked around the pommel of the saddle. Later, no doubt spurred on by the desire to find a safer seat, she took the idea one step further, adding an extra horn to the top of the nearside of her saddle so that she could wedge her right knee between the two pommels. It was a brilliant concept, giving her far greater security (though nothing like as secure as the modern side saddle), and one which, remarkably, remained the basic structure of the side saddle for another 250 years.

When Catherine first began riding with her leg over the pommel of her saddle its seems to have caused quite a stir in the hunting field, and Brantôme, perhaps maliciously, wrote that she had done it not for security but out of vanity. 'The Dauphiness was very good indeed on horseback and strong, and held herself very gracefully having been the first who had put her leg in the arch of the saddle, so that it looked much more graceful and pleasing than the footboard. The desire to show her leg was one reason for the invention, because she had very nice ones, her calves being well formed, and she took pleasure in well booting herself, and of seeing her *chausse* [stockings and breeches all in one] well put on, and not wrinkled. With this she wore a manteau of black velvet, a big apron of the same material covering the front of the saddle, and descending below the housings [trappings of the saddle] which were short and decorated with big hanging balls of silk, and her left leg being tucked up under the said apron gripping the saddle.'

Catherine may have been vain, but she was clearly a brave, hard-riding woman, and the additional security helped her to enjoy hunting until she was sixty, although it is said that she never understood the finer points of venery as Anne de Beaujeu and Diane de Poitier had before her. It was in the court of Catherine and Henri II that the young Mary, Queen of Scots, grew up, having been sent there at the age of five by her mother, on the understanding that she would eventually marry Catherine's four-year-old weakling son, Francis. Mary would have known Diane de Poitiers, for among her many accomplishments at the court, which included learning Latin, Spanish, Italian and Greek, and enjoying a taste for music and poetry, she excelled at hunting and dancing. There was also the scandal of her English governess, Lady Fleming, who, much to the fury of both Catherine de Medici and Diane de Poitiers, became one of Henri II's lovers. When she was indiscreet enough to become pregnant, the two women combined to oust her, and she was sent home in disgrace.

For Mary, who was rapidly growing into a tall, slender beauty, it must have been a charmed childhood, probably the happiest days of her tragic life. Within two years of her marriage to Francis, at the age of eighteen, Mary found herself a widow ruling over a divided and unwelcoming Scotland. There then followed her disastrous marriage to the Earl of Darnley, whose plot to imprison her and her unborn child was thwarted when she escaped on horseback from Holyrood Palace. She was six months' pregnant and had to ride for five hours. Two years later, having married Darnley's murderer, Bothwell, and been forced to abdicate in favour of her baby son, Mary sought refuge in England, where she became a prisoner of Elizabeth I for eighteen years. She was executed in 1587 at the age of forty-four.

By the middle of the sixteenth century it was becoming increasingly less acceptable for women to ride astride, both in England and on the Continent. Fynes Moryson, writing at the beginning of the seventeenth century, was obviously quite shocked by the sight of women riding in this fashion:

'Also I have seene honourable Women, as well married as Virgines, ride by the high way in Princes traines, apparrelled like Men, in a doublet close to the body, and large breeches open at the knees, after the Spanish fashion, both of carnation silke or satten, and likewise riding astride like men upon Horses and Mules, but their heads were attired like Women, with bare haires knotted, or else covered with gold netted cawles, and a hat with a feather.'

Women who did ride astride in the seventeenth and eighteenth centuries were generally deplored, but such notions of etiquette would not have deterred France's most outrageous Queen Consort, Marie Antoinette. This high-spirited wife of the inadequate, ugly King Louis XVI was said to be 'frivolous, imprudent and prodigal, and an enemy of reform,' who 'contributed to the popular unrest that led to the Revolution and the overthrow of the monarchy in August 1792.'[2] Her wild extravagances added an extra burden to the huge debt incurred by the French State in the 1770s and '80s, and her close association with the more dissipated members of Louis XVI's court gave her enemies ample opportunity to spread rumours about extramarital affairs. She was, however, a good horsewoman. In 1775 she was seen hunting 'riding side saddle on a grey horse and wearing a shovel hat with plumes', and it was noticed 'how dangerous and vicious-looking were the hunters she and her ladies rode.'[3] Sometimes she rode astride, on a saddle covered with a leopard skin, and 'dressed like a man in green pantaloons and an English riding–coat and round hat.' Her behaviour shocked the French aristocracy as well as antagonising the poorer people at a time when France's monarchy was already on shaky ground. Headstrong and misguided, but not without supporters, she was sent to the guillotine a year after the Revolution.

Among other notorious huntresses of the age was Lady Lade, who, before her marriage to Sir John Lade, was said to have been the mistress of a highwayman. A renowned society beauty and brilliant horsewoman, she is thought to have inspired the creation of the R. S. Surtees character, Lucy Glitters, the gay and fearless huntress who captured the heart of Mr Sponge. In the Royal Buckhounds 'run of the season' in 1799, which lasted two hours and forty minutes, it is reported that 'Lady Lade kept up the whole time . . . her fleet courser never failed.'

The first woman to take office as Master of the Foxhounds was the Marchioness of Salisbury, who established the Hatfield Hunt in 1775. A daunting task for a woman of the eighteenth century, but Lady Salisbury was, by all accounts, unlikely to allow anyone or anything to hold her back. Ostentatious and domineering, she dressed exotically, entertained on a lavish scale, and 'liked to float down the river in a barge attended by a dozen liveried menservants, or drive round the estate throwing golden guineas to the tenants.'[4] Apart from hunting, she enjoyed driving a four-in-hand team and practising archery. She was an exceptionally brave rider across country, never failing to keep up with her hounds, which were noted for their steadiness and fine noses. She continued hunt-

Laetitia, Lady Lade, by George Stubbs.

ing until she was well past seventy, by which time she was so blind that she had to be strapped to the saddle and guided by a groom with a leading rein who would shout: 'Damn you, my Lady, Jump!' whenever they reached a fence. Her death was as dramatic as her life had been. It is thought that the feathers in her hair caught alight in the flame of a candle, causing a fire that destroyed her and the entire west wing of Hatfield House.

Most of the records of women riding in the fourteenth to eighteenth centuries tended to be of those connected to the Royal courts, since they were of greatest interest to historians. Few women, with the exception of those in the hunting field, were recorded solely for their achievements on horseback, but one who has made a place for herself in historical records, through her enthusiasm of riding, is Celia Fiennes. *Through England on a Side Saddle in the time of William and Mary* was the title of the diary she wrote between 1685 and 1703. Born in Newton Toney, near Salisbury, in 1662, an age when a woman's activities were severely restricted to home and family, Celia Fiennes was clearly an unconventional character. Her journeys were undertaken, she explains, 'for the sake of health', but its seems more likely that they were to satisfy an inquisitive nature and a desire for action. The

A Hawking Party by James Ross.

records of her travels all over the country are extraordinary in their detail, and she succeeded in creating a picture of seventeenth century England which the historian G. M. Trevelyan regarded as 'a valuable source of economic and social history, in the same class as Defoe's *Tour* a few years later.'

Travelling mostly by horseback with a handful of servants, she negotiated roads and tracks that were impassable by wheeled vehicles (in Fen country her horse nearly fell into a dyke beside a flooded causeway), and found her way around the countryside surprisingly well at a time when signposts were only just coming into use. Travellers losing their way received little help from the natives, who knew 'scarce three mile from their home'. Sometimes she would stay with friends and relatives, other times in the local inns. These were noisy and 'so crowded that three must lye in a bed.' In Ely she found 'froggs and slow-worms and snailes in my roome.' In Cheshire she was waylaid by highwaymen: 'two fellows . . . truss'd up with great coates and as it were bundles about them which I believe was pistolls.' She escaped from this ordeal unharmed, and ventured into Scotland, then a country where no one, according to Macaulay, went without first making his will. She even travelled among the 'barefoote . . . nasty sort of people' of Wales.

Her interests spanned from crawling through caves in Derbyshire to trade and industry, the quality and price of food, types of agriculture, soil type and fertility, and she gives detailed architectural notes and comments on a variety of buildings including cathedrals and ancestral homes. The diaries record everything she saw and did, in a direct if somewhat unorthodox style, with scant regard for spelling and punctuation. They are the result of an extraordinary undertaking by a woman with energy and initiative, and with a lively and enquiring mind.

Apart from some of the cross saddle exceptions mentioned, women continued to ride side saddle, using Catherine de Medici's extra pommel, but in 1830 a French riding master, Jules Pellier, invented the leaping head. This was another horn fixed to the saddle

Queen Elizabeth I in the hunting field. A woodcut from G. Turberville's *Booke of Venerie*, 1572.

just above the left thigh, so that the rider could grip upwards with her left leg while the right remained firmly held between the two top pommels. It was this invention – by far the greatest advance in side saddle riding – that gave women such security. They could now cope, even more adeptly than male riders astride, with any movement that would tend to pitch them over their horse's head. It is surprising that such an invention was so long in arriving: throughout the Renaissance the practice of 'classical' riding had been developing, and by the eighteenth century had reached new heights of refinement. Horsemanship had become an essential accomplishment for a gentleman, and the great riding masters of *haute école* – Grisone, Pignatelli, La Broue and de Pluvinel – had already made their mark. Yet scant attention had been paid to improving the lot of the equestrienne.

Fortunately for the Renaissance woman the pace of hunting was not as fast as it is today – indeed, it was often little more than a stately procession. A contemporary description of Queen Elizabeth I and her hunting cavalcade in 1557 (just before her accession) gives some idea of the pomp and ceremony that occasioned such events. 'In April she was escorted from Hatfield to Enfield Chase by a retinue of twelve ladies clothed in white satin, on ambling palfreys and twenty yeomen in green, all on horseback, that Her Grace might hunt the hart.' Quite apart from the insecurity of their saddles, women were further hampered by their extravagant clothes, and it is often difficult to ascertain exactly what they were sitting on beneath their voluminous petticoats and skirts.

The riding masters of the Renaissance gave little thought to improving the techniques of side saddle riding until the publication of a book in 1770 entitled *Le Nouveau Parfait Mareschal*, by Francois de Garsault. The book devotes considerable space to the lady rider, and illustrates the correct position for a woman in the side saddle. Some thirty years later, in his book *Scuola Equestre*, Federico Mazzuchelli offers this wonderful advice on mounting:

'Although the lady will presumably have studied the masculine way of reaching the saddle, as described in the previous chapter, it will be necessary for her to get closer to the horse and stand more squarely to the stirrup. Moreover, instead of swinging her right leg over the horse's rump she should, at the instant in which she finds herself standing in the stirrup on her left foot, draw away slightly from the saddle, and turning the body in a quarter circle to the left, pass her right leg between the horse's body and her left leg, so as to raise her right thigh and place the knee firmly in the fork – all of which movements are aided by the right hand which, after serving as a lifting force, should leave the cantle in favour of the right fork so as to contribute to balancing the body while, turning, it takes its place in the saddle.'

The advent of the leaping head was to revolutionise riding for women, for now they were able to take on the faster pace of hunting in relative safety. But, in Britain, the invention had arrived at a time when women had never been less welcome in the hunting field, and it took many years for them to benefit from its introduction.

CHAPTER TWO
THE SOCIALITES

'When women do ride they generally ride like the very devil.'
R. S. Surtees, (1803–1864), *Analysis of the Hunting Field*

Throughout the seventeenth and eighteenth centuries women had displayed great courage and skill in the hunting field. Huntresses like Catherine de Medici, Lady Lade and the Marchioness of Salisbury had become reknowned equestriennes, easily capable of keeping pace with the men. Their feats were all the more remarkable when one considers what they were up against: saddles that offered so little security that a balancing act was needed to stay in position, and voluminous skirts that were always getting in the way. It is extraordinary that, instead of making things easier for themselves, the women of the early nineteenth century chose to wear riding outfits that were even more impracticable, and often downright dangerous. Long, flowing skirts, which trailed close to the ground, would frighten the horses and could easily become tangled around the saddle should the rider fall. Hats were often large and exotic, with veils or fancy plumes – very decorative but not very sensible.

John Wootton's painting of the Countess of Oxford in 1716 shows her wearing a scarlet habit of which the skirt is cut along a straight line just below the foot. In 1770 the French riding master, Francois de Garsault, was advocating a skirt short enough to show both feet and for the rider's hair to be tied neatly under a small hat. Yet within forty years the extravagances of the Regency period in England had manifested themselves in absurd outfits that were totally impracticable for cross country riding. Social etiquette was also to blame. In the early nineteenth century no women would have considered wearing breeches under her skirt, but because she had to avoid exposing her ankles, it was necessary to wear layers of petticoats and long skirts, and to take endless trouble to ensure that the garments stayed in place. It was a time, however, when few women hunted for, despite

The Countess of Oxford
by John Wootton,
1716.

the courageous exploits of some of their sex, their position in the hunting world was weakening. Two factors had combined to bring this about. In the second half of the eighteenth century it had become fashionable among the sportsmen in the Shires to gallop over their fences, and since the Enclosure Acts were coming into force, the fences erected to contain livestock were often formidable. Women who, in the past, had managd to jump obstacles at a much slower pace, probably by hanging on to the back of the saddle with one hand, found it almost impossible to tackle the huge fences that they encountered so fast and frequently.

The second factor was a changing social climate in which it became less and less acceptable for women to appear in hunting circles. Hunting had become a different sort of sport – faster, more dangerous and often more disreputable. During the winter season the Shires would be invaded by wild young men wanting to partake in the excitement of the sport; it was a bachelor life and women were not welcomed. Soon the only women who were accepted in the hunting field were those with some connection to the hunt – wives and daughters of the Master, for example. Any others would have been regarded as women of doubtful virtue. So when, in 1830, the Frenchman Jules Charles Pellier invented the leaping head, an addition to the side saddle which, as already explained, gave far greater

Amazone. Mme L. Montant Monte-Cristo, Cheval Anglais pur Sang, by Pierre Jules Mène (1865) and (*below*) *Interior of a riding school* by F. C. Turner, 1843.

security, women in Britain were slow to take advantage of it, and it did not come into general use for another thirty years. It did, nonetheless, enable those women who were bold or brazen enough to go hunting to tackle the huge fences as safely and competently as the men. This was an era when only a handful of women genuinely hunted (many would attend the meets on horseback, but not follow the hounds), and their presence in the hunting field caused a good deal of comment, not always favourable.

'Women *have* no business out hunting,' wrote R. S. Surtees in 1858 (*Ask Mama*), though he did concede that they had a beneficial influence on the coarse speech and even coarser habits of the foxhunters. Anthony Trollope in his *Hunting Sketches*, published in 1865, was more welcoming: 'Their presence tends to take off from hunting that character of horseyness . . . which has become, not unnaturally, attached to it, and to bring it within the category of gentle sports.' He was also of the view that 'Women who ride, as a rule, ride better than men', but was careful to remind the hunting lady that 'no man ever likes a woman to know as much about a horse as he thinks he knows himself.'

The debate on whether or not women should hunt was obviously a heated one. Those who disapproved thought up all sorts of reasons why ladies should not partake, one being that it exposed them to improper behaviour. 'It leads to flirting, they say – to flirting of a sort which mothers would not approve, and it leads to fast habits.' Women who did hunt were frequently the subject of malicious gossip, but they were also an inspiration to many contemporary writers. G. J. Whyte-Melville's character Cissy Dove 'could ride with a degree of nerve and judgement seldom enjoyed by the softer sex', and R. S. Surtees' pretty heroine Lucy Glitters set a dashing pace across country. Romance in the hunting field was rife.

'. . . he made his way to Miss Glitters with the brush, exclaiming, "We'll put this in your hat, alongside the cock's feathers".

The fair lady leant towards him, and as he adjusted it becomingly in her hat, looking in her bewitching eyes, her lovely face, and feeling the soft fragrance of her breath, a something shot through Mr Sponge's pull-devil, pull-baker coat, his corduroy waistcoat, his Eureka shirt, Angola vest and penetrated the very cockles of his heart. He gave her such a series of smacking kisses as startled her horse and astonished a poacher who happened to be hid in the adjoining hedge.'

Whatever the feelings on the rights and wrongs of women hunting, one certain fact is that any woman who rode well, however dubious her background or her motives for going hunting, was greatly admired. Exceptionally good horsemanship could provide an entrée into the elite hunting circles of the fashionable Shires, in spite of the rigid social barriers that existed in those days. 'The English sportsman's love of a horse, and his admiration for horsemanship, made it impossible for him to reject anyone whose talent in this sphere was outstanding. If a woman could appear in the hunting field and look magnificent, and could then ride with courage, grace and artistry, the social barriers were apt to

The Riding School by Edmond Grandjean. Until the nineteenth century little attention was given to improving the art of equestrianism for women.

(*above*) *A Hunting Incident* by Thomas Rowlandson, about 1795.

(*below*) *Emma Anne Mortimer riding her favourite hunter on the seashore* by J. F. Herring Snr, 1842.

(*above*) Lucy Glitters in R. S. Surtees' *Mr Sponge's Sporting Tour*, and (*right*) Cissy Dove, the heroine of G. J. Whyte-Melville's *Market Harborough*.

Cissy Dove

Miss de Glancey captivates the Earl, from R. S. Surtees' *Ask Mama*.

crumble.'[5] It was for this reason that a poor girl from Liverpool was able to penetrate the highest echelons of a close-knit Victorian Society.

Catherine Walters was born on 13 June 1839, near the Mersey riverfront in Liverpool. He father worked for HM Customs, and it said that Catherine gained her nickname 'Skittles' because she used to earn money setting up the skittles in a public house near her home. Quite how a girl from her background learnt to ride as well as she did is not known; one story is that she worked in a circus as a bare-back rider. Most probably she had access to a local livery stables and helped out there, exercising horses and teaching herself to ride by watching others. Clearly, she had a natural talent as a horsewoman, and when, in the late 1850s, she moved to London, she was already a proficient rider.

Her 'career' as a member of the notorious demimonde took off after a chance meeting with a man who ran a livery stable at the back of Park Lane. Not long after this she became Lord Hartington's mistress, and, following some fortuitous publicity in *The Times*, was soon the most famous courtesan in London. That she was able to make such a name for herself in high circles was the result of an extraordinary paradox of morals that existed in the Victorian era: society would have been appalled by the sight of a beautiful young prostitute soliciting on foot in Hyde Park, but a prostitute on a horse was somehow different. 'Her passport was her poise in the saddle.'[5]

By the second half of the nineteenth century riding and driving in Rotten Row had become as much a part of the 'season' as Ascot and Henley. It was the parade ground of the rich and fashionable, where everyone rode on the best and most expensive hacks they could afford. It was also the hunting ground of the demimonde. 'The Danaes! The Amazons! The lady cavaliers! The horse-women!' wrote George Augustus Sala. 'Can any scene in the world equal Rotten Row at four in the afternoon and in the full tide of the season? Watch the sylphides as they fly or float past in their ravishing riding-habits and intoxicatingly delightful hats; . . . Those are not all countesses' or earls' daughters, my son . . . Some of these dashing delightful creatures have covered themselves with shame, and their mothers with grief, and have brought their fathers' grey hair with sorrow to the grave. All is not gold that glitters, my son.'

'Skittles' – Catherine Walters – the nineteenth-century courtesan who first made a name for herself riding in Hyde Park.

Owners of livery stables were well aware of the benefits of showing off their animals in the hands of an attractive, elegant girl, so when the dealer at Bruton Mews discovered that Catherine Walters was an excellent horsewoman as well as an outstanding beauty, he was quick to employ her. She was taken to one of the best tailors in London to be fitted with the latest habit, and it is said that it was tailored to fit her figure so closely that she could wear nothing underneath. Riding out every day in Hyde Park, she soon became recognised as one of the 'pretty horse-breakers', but as well as good looks and good horsemanship, Catherine was clearly a woman of intelligence and guile, whose pride never allowed her to sell herself cheaply or to a man she disliked. It was in Hyde Park in 1862 that she met Lord Hartington, the eldest son of the 7th Duke of Devonshire, who was then aged twenty-eight and a bachelor. Their affair soon became known in society, but later that year another event occurred that gave Catherine even greater publicity.

The Times published a letter, written under a pseudonym, that was a blatant reference to Catherine Walters and the interest she had created in the Park. The letter blamed the traffic congestion of the South Carriage Road, which had been particularly bad at that time, not on the number of people travelling to and from the popular International Exhibition at Kensington, but on the presence of a young horsewoman who chose either to ride or drive during the rush hour, and whose appearance caused such a sensation that it halted the traffic in both directions. The publication of the letter resulted in Catherine becoming one of the most talked of women in London Society. Suddenly it was Catherine that everyone wanted to copy. Whatever she wore became the latest style, and wherever she chose to ride became the most popular place to promenade.

The young swells in Rotton Row
  All cut it mighty fine,
And quiz the fair sex, you know,
  And say it is divine.
The pretty little horse-breakers
  Are breaking hearts like fun,
For in Rotton Row they all must go
  The whole hog or none.

Her short, traumatic affair with Lord Hartington ended on a sour note, though Catherine received a substantial life settlement from the Devonshire estate. She then went to Paris for some years, soon conquering Parisian society. Count Albert de Maugny described Catherine in his memoirs: 'She had fair hair in a natural blonde shade; her eyes were deep blue, her complexion dazzling, her features sculptured in an admirable purity of line, her waist slender, her deportment aristocratic . . . And what perfect taste she possessed! What elegance! What grace on horseback!'

In the winter Catherine would return to Britain and base herself at the Haycock Inn

at Wansford for the hunting season. Her presence was at first strongly resented, and there were many who never really accepted her, but she soon found enough friends and admirers among the hunting set to defend her. She went out of her way to avoid causing offence and embarrassment, and always refused invitations to visit or stay in a private house. One story goes that at a meet of the Quorn where Catherine had appeared, Lady Stamford, wife of the Master, created quite a scene, telling her husband that either he sent Catherine home or she would go home herself and never hunt with the Quorn again. Catherine, overhearing the threat, immediately left, but on her way home, hounds in full cry crossed her path and she could not resist rejoining the hunt. It is said that she rode so straight and well that at the end of the run Lord Stamford came up to congratulate her and to tell her that she would always be welcome to hunt with the Quorn. When Catherine asked him about Lady Stamford, he replied 'Damn all jealous women!'.

Among the many fashions set by Catherine, she is credited with introducing the silk hat and veil. By now the riding habits worn by women had become considerably more practicable. Skirts were shorter and neater, with few, if any, petticoats. 'All superfluity of under-clothing should be dispensed with both for convenience in riding as well as for personal appearance' wrote Mrs J. Stirling Clarke in *The Habit and the Horse* (1857). 'At the same time, the error of extremes which some ladies run, by the absence of all petticoats, must be carefully avoided. Few indeed look well, shorn of these necessary appendages to the equestrian costume.'

'Skittles' remained the unrivalled Queen of the Chase for many seasons, but by 1876 when the Empress of Austria first made her appearance in the hunting field, Catherine was past her prime. She had set up a permanent home for herself in Chesterfield Street, London, where she enjoyed the companionship of many friends and admirers, including the Prince of Wales, Gladstone, and Sir Wilfrid Blunt. She remained in London for the rest of her life, dying on 5 August 1920.

Had it not been for her association with the horse, Catherine Walters would probably never have made a name for herself in such an elite society. There were no such social barriers to be overcome by the Empress of Austria, but it was still the horse that gave her the greatest joy in her tragic life. The Bavarian-born Elizabeth, whose childhood had been carefree and wild, rebelled against the stultifying atmosphere of the Austrian court in which she found herself following her marriage to her cousin Franz Joseph, Emperor of Austria. At odds with her mother-in-law and devastated by the death of her eldest daughter from measles, she took solace in riding. She began hunting in Hungary, and spent much time studying *haute école* and improving her horsemanship. Well before the introduction of Caprilli's forward seat over fences, she noted that 'one must throw the body forward at the take-off.'

She arrived in England in March 1876 to hunt with the Grafton. It was the Golden

Rotten Row in The Season, from *The Graphic*, 8 July 1871.

Age of hunting in England, and there was nothing comparable in Austria to the open fields and the big hedges and ditches over which the British huntsmen rode at such a breath-

The Empress of Austria and her Pilot, a sketch published in *The Illustrated Sporting and Dramatic News*, 19 March 1881.

taking pace. For this reason the Empress came to visit the Shires, and following a successful outing in Grafton country she was invited to join the Pytchley. It was customary in those days for hunting women to have a pilot, a good male rider who would guide her over the fences, choose the most suitable routes, and ensure that she was always safe and well looked after. The Empress's pilot, Bay Middleton, was the epitome of the sporting gentlemen of that era. Born to a hunting background, he soon earned a reputation for being the fastest and straightest man across the country, and was chosen to be the 'hunting'

ADC to Lord Spencer in Ireland. He was good-looking, charming and high-spirited, a successful steeplechase rider and good cricketer. When the Empress came to England Lord Spencer was the Master of the Pytchley, and he asked Middleton to be the Empress's pilot. The request was not greeted with enthusiasm. For Middleton the pleasure of hunting was to be able to lead 'the cream of the cream in the shire of shires', and the last thing he wanted was to be encumbered by a woman. He grudgingly agreed to his task.

Middleton need not have worried. The Empress, encouraging him to take his own line at his own pace, followed by him without hesitation and never failed to keep up. 'This perfect man to hounds [was] followed by the best and most beautiful horsewoman that ever lived, their horses in perfect balance, taking each fence just as it came in a run,' according to Charles Kinsky, one of Elizabeth's Hungarian friends. Although nine years his senior, the Empress was clearly enchanted by Middleton, and for four seasons he was her pilot, both in England and Ireland.

> *The Queen! Yes, the Empress!*
> *Look how she flies.*
> *With a hand that ne'er fails*
> *And a pluck that ne'er dies.*
> *Hark horn and Hark holloa!*
> *Cram on for a place!*
> *He must ride who would follow*
> *The Queen of the Chase*

The daring pace of the Empress and her closeness to Middleton were soon the talk of the sporting drawing rooms, but in 1881, Middleton announced his plans to marry Charlotte Baird, to whom he had been unofficially engaged before he ever met the Empress. Elizabeth felt betrayed. With the loss of her favourite pilot and increasing age, her enthusiasm for hunting dwindled. She had been her happiest in the hunting field, revelling in the excitement and the admiration that it brought her, and frequently flaunting her court duties in favour of the chase. Now that had come to an end, and she never hunted in England again. In Austria she may not have heard of Middleton's tragic death at a Warwickshire point-to-point in 1892, for her own life was fraught with despair. The death of her cousin, King Ludwig of Bavaria, was followed by her son's suicide at Mayerling. In September 1898 the Empress was shot through the heart by an assassin as she boarded a steamer on the lake of Geneva.

Her appearance in the hunting field in Britain had caused a sensation. Not only had she quickly become renowned for her skilled riding across country, but she was both beautiful and charming. She was always immaculately turned out, wearing a smooth chamois leather bodice under a habit into which she had to be sewn. Guy Paget wrote: 'The presence of the Empress was not an unmixed blessing. The field grew to unmanageable numbers, five hundred being counted upon one occasion; flocks of strangers arriving to gaze upon this vision of royal beauty while ambitious males rode to catch her eye with more courage than discretion.'[6]

Elizabeth had set a precedent for women to hunt again, and throughout the 1880s their numbers increased dramatically. Their invasion of the hunting field sometimes caused complaint, particularly of those women who rode badly or appeared to have little understanding of the finer points of hunting, but it also brought to the equestrienne's attention the need

Lady Clifford's Harriers. A photograph from *Country Life*, 12 March 1898.

for a number of improvements in their equipment. The third pommel, on the off-side of the side saddle, had gradually been dwindling away, until by the 1880s it had disappeared altogether. This opened the way for radical changes to the construction of the saddle itself: the tree of the saddle was cut back in a half-circle over the withers, enabling unnecessary

An Elegant Lady riding in a park with her spaniels by Alfred de Dreux (1814–1860).

An Elegant Equestrienne on a Grey by Alfred de Dreux.

Queen Victoria on Horseback, 1838 by Sir Edwin Henry Landseer.

(*above*) *Mrs J. Burden of Syosset, Long Island* by Sir Alfred Munnings.

(*below*) *A Summer Hack on Exmoor ; Lady Violet Munnings on Magnolia* by Sir Alfred Munnings.

padding (an unwelcome feature of early side saddles) to be removed, and allowing the rider's leg to come in closer contact with the horse. As well as providing a more comfortable position for the rider, it also reduced the excessive weight of the saddle, which was often the cause of sore backs on horses.

The stirrups also underwent changes, and various forms of 'safety' stirrups were introduced to allow the foot to be released in the event of a fall. The concept of the safety stirrup did not meet with universal approval, however, as they could not be guaranteed to work. Mrs Power O'Donoghue, an 'authority on female equitation', who contributed articles to *The Illustrated Sporting and Dramatic News* in the 1880s, gave the following advice to women: 'If the horse should at any time run away with you, keep your seat whilst you *can* do so; . . . but if there is any danger of you being thrown or losing your seat whilst your foot is caught, then by all means ride for a fall; and put your horse at something that will bring him down, and when he *is* down struggle onto his head, that he may not rise until somebody has come to your assistance. Of course the experiment is fraught with excessive danger, but it is not *certain* death, as the other alternative must undoubtedly be.'

Woman Riding Side Saddle, a bronze by De Crepi.

In 1889 Mrs O'Donoghue published a book entitled *Ladies on Horseback*, which she wrote because of her 'disappointment with the riding ability and turnout of many ladies, both in the hunting field and in Rotten Row'. Aspiring socialites, anxious to join the riding and hunting circles, would appear on horseback wrongly attired, riding badly, and displaying an obvious lack of knowledge. In short, they were giving the female rider a bad name. Mrs O'Donoghue's instructions on dress were quite clear: 'Skirt to reach six inches below the foot, well shaped for the knee, and neatly shotted at end of hem just below the right foot; elastic band upon inner side, to catch the left toe, and to retain the skirt in its place. It should be made tight and spare, without *one inch* of superfluous cloth; jacket close fitting, but sufficiently easy to avoid the suspicion of being squeezed; sleeves perfectly tight, except at the setting on, where a slight puffiness over the shoulder should give the appearance of increased width of chest. A small neat linen collar, upright shape, with cuffs to correspond, should be worn with the habit, no frilling or fancy work being admissable – the collar to be fastened with a plain gold or silver stud.' Her book then goes on to describe – over another seven pages – how the riding clothes should be put on.

Such was the emphasis on correct dress at this time that a number of tailors in London began specialising in riding outfits; they would provide a room where a woman could sit on a wooden horse to try out her habit. Before the introduction of the apron skirt at the turn of the century, women wore 'safety' skirts, which had a slit behind that had to be hastily fastened together after dismounting. Apparently the skirt was first worn in England in 1875 by Mrs Arthur of Market Harborough, who shocked her friends when she appeared out hunting in the garment. But when women began wearing breeches and riding boots, it was much easier to do away with superfluous material in the skirt, and the 'apron' which was subsequently introduced soon gained general approval.

No sooner had the side saddle and all its accoutrements been perfected than its very use began to be questioned. There developed a strong anti-side saddle lobby who voiced a number of complaints, some justified some not, denigrating the side saddle. It was, they argued, a heavy and cumbersome piece of equipment that was difficult for a woman to handle and had to be girthed up by a groom; it caused sore backs on the horses and it was uncomfortable for the rider, being blamed for the serious backaches suffered by some women after a long day's hunting. Its impracticalities were aggravated by a changing social climate in which fewer women could afford grooms to prepare their hunters, to help them mount and to provide second horses.

Final Position, a sketch from S. Sidney's *Book of the Horse* (1874). In deference to the female form, the side saddle position has been illustrated by a man's legs.

The most serious complaint, however, was that the side saddle was dangerous. The leaping head, which had been such a welcome addition to the saddle in the middle of the nineteenth century, had given the rider almost too much security. If a horse came down, its rider was unlikely to be thrown clear, and many serious accidents befell women who became trapped between their horse and the ground, or who were dragged with their foot caught in the stirrup. Golden Gorse (Muriel Wace), author of *Moorland Mousie* and *The Young Rider*, and one of the pioneers of riding astride, claimed that 'I should prefer three falls astride to one sideways, and I have considerable experience of both.'

The seeds of discontent had already been sown by the turn of the century, but initially the idea of women riding astride was greeted with outrage. According to Meriel Buxton, 'Lord Annaly, Master of the Pytchley from 1902 to 1914, was particularly outspoken in his disapproval of the practice and went so far as to refuse to give the Pytchley white collar to any woman who rode astride.'[7] Belle Beach, in her book *Riding and Driving for Women*, published in 1912, made her views quite clear: 'I deplore the tendency and believe that it is a mere passing fad . . . the average woman is not built for cross saddle riding . . . and looks ridiculous and immodest in this position.' While Mrs Hayes, another contemporary author, had even stronger words on the subject: 'Anyone who takes up this idea seriously must be either mad or wholly ignorant.'

Yet by 1907 the concept of riding astride had already received credence in *Country Life*,

(*above*) A bad fall in the show jumping arena. The most serious complaint made of the side saddle was that women were not thrown clear of their horse in a fall. (*right*) Edith Somerville, author and MFH, from a *Country Life* frontispiece, 1920.

whose fashion pages extolled the virtues of the latest 'ride astride' habits: 'Nothing could be more graceful and charming in appearance than the long coat, hanging straight at each side and just disclosing the boot, and when dismounted the effect is far neater than an ordinary habit with the irregular length of the two sides of the skirt. No wonder that riding astride, with the far safer seat it gives a woman, is coming more and more into favour when our tailors show how far more becoming the long riding coat is than the skin-tight habit skirt.'

The arguments continued. In 1922 there was heated correspondence in *Horse and Hound* on the subject. A letter published on 1 July complained that, of the ten entrants in the Ladies' Hunter classes at the Richmond Horse Show, seven were selected to be judged and the remainder sent out. All those kept in the ring were riding side saddle, and the remaining three 'outcasts' were astride.

'Can Ladies Ride Astride?' was the title of an article by Lt Col M. F. Taggart published in *Country Life* in April 1924. Also in favour of the new trend, he dispelled many of the arguments made against it, one of these being that because women tend to have round thighs they were not designed to ride astride. He points out that 'the muscles of all thighs are flat when the leg is bent and the sinews tightened.' However, on the argument that women have knock-knees and, therefore, have more difficulty riding astride than men, he merely comments: 'Far be it from me to express an opinion upon so delicate a subject.'

It was also said that a woman, being of the weaker sex, could not have a strong enough grip on a horse when riding astride. 'This argument might have something in it were horsemanship a matter of sheer strength but . . . It is so much a question of balance.' Col Taggart went on to praise the ability of women: 'It seems to me that ladies possess naturally the qualities of horsemanship more than men . . . They grasp the rhythm and cadence, and balance seems to come naturally to them . . . The delicacy of touch and the sympathy which is a necessity for good hands are both feminine attributes.' To support his case he quoted as an example Lady Wright's successes in the show jumping world. Unlike most of her contemporaries, both on the Continent and in England, Lady Wright always rode astride, and was already competing at international shows by the time Col Taggart wrote his article. Women were also riding in point-to-points at this time, some astride and some side saddle, but it would be many years before the traditionalists gave way to the 'new' form of riding.

One of the firm supporters of the side saddle was Mrs Archer Houblon, who for nineteen years prepared HM The Queen's horse for her Birthday Parade. As late as 1938, when the majority of women had changed over to riding astride, Mrs Houblon published a book devoted entirely to the art of riding side saddle. Her view was that many of the faults attributed to the side saddle, in particular sore backs on horses, were caused by bad riding. Because the side saddle offers such a secure seat, many women felt quite at ease after only a few rides, and thought they had nothing more to learn. It was these riders who created the problems, not the saddles.

Competitor at the Side Saddle Association's annual show. In the last fifteen years there has been renewed interest in the side saddle.

Although there were some who remained faithful to the side saddle, Mrs Houblon's book must have fallen mostly on deaf ears. Yet fifty years later, women were again turning the tables to such an extent that J. A. Allen considered it worthwhile to revise and update the book for re-publication; attics were scoured for grandmother's old riding habits, and the makers of side saddles were back in business. In 1974 there was enough interest to warrant the formation of the Side Saddle Association, an organisation that has gone from strength to strength and now has over 1,000 members. Why should so many people want to revive a mode of riding that most of their forbears were only too glad to discard?

Sheer vanity is one answer. There is no doubt that the elegance of a woman riding side saddle is one of its greatest attractions, but it does not stop there. There are some riders who, for reasons of physical disability, are unable to ride astride, but can manage happily on a side saddle. Others find that the additional security offered by the side saddle gives them the confidence they lacked astride. For many it simply adds another, enjoyable, dimension to a variety of riding activities.

However, for the women who wanted to make the most of the increasing number of opportunities to compete in equestrian sports, from eventing and racing to polo and endurance riding, the side saddle had definitely had its day. This awkward little verse, written by Emily Stevens in the guest book of Lida Fleitmann Bloodgood in about 1918, makes clear her feelings on the subject.

U is for us when united we fight
That the skirt called divided be worn by the fair
If you've seen a dear girl with her boots in the air,
When she lands in a furrow, you'll know I'm right.

CHAPTER THREE
SHOW JUMPING

Show jumping is a sport still dominated by men. Numerically, they easily outweigh women, and they have won the majority of international championships. But, considering the disadvantage of numbers – only three of the sixty riders at the 1984 Olympics were female, for example – women who have competed at the top levels of this sport have done exceptionally well.

In the 1968, '72 and '76 Olympics the sole representatives of the female sex on the British show jumping team, Marion Coakes, Ann Moore and Debbie Johnsey respectively, each gained better results than their teammates in the individual competition, and Marion Coakes and Ann Moore both won individual silver medals, an achievement unequalled by any British man up to 1988. Although no woman has won the European title since the amalgamation of the men's and women's championship in 1975, the Canadian rider, Gail Greenough, became the first woman to win the World Championships in 1980. On numerical grounds, the odds against a victory for a woman at those championships were 10 to 1.

It is surprising that women have not made a greater impact on this sport, because they were involved with it, albeit in a small way, from its early days at the turn of this century. Having already shown their prowess in the hunting field, it was only natural that they should extend their abilities to the jumping arena, since most of the earlier competitions were organised as a test for hunters. The jumps resembled cross country obstacles, rather than the coloured fences of today. Banks, stone walls and ditches were all a part of the jumping competitions held at the Dublin Horse Show, which began at Leinster Lawn in 1864. The show moved to its present site at Ballsbridge in 1891 (where there is still a bank to be jumped), and two years later the first National Horse Show was staged at the old Madison Garden in New York. This show soon established itself as a major event in America's social calendar, and it was here that one of that country's most talented women

47

Women tent-pegging at a gymkhana, 1929.

Lida Fleitmann (née Bloodgood) riding Palmetto. One of the most outstanding women riders in America at the beginning of this century.

(*above*) Team gold medallist Melanie Smith riding Calypso at the Los Angeles Olympic Games in 1984.

(*below*) The victorious all-female American team at the 1987 Hickstead Nations Cup competition.

Top British woman show jumper : Liz Edgar on Everest Forever.

riders first made a name for herself.

'Perhaps my proudest moment at The Garden', wrote Mrs J. Van S. Bloodgood, 'was when [in 1918] . . . I won the Ladies' Team class with my three chestnuts: Longwood, shown by that consummate horsewoman Margaret Thorne Carle (later MFH of the Mill-brook), Winchester, ridden by Annette Robinson, and myself on Palmetto, with whom I had won many a triple bar jump and championship.'[8]

Lida Bloodgood (née Fleitmann) was an outstanding horsewoman. She had numerous successes in the show ring, both in America and England, became a renowned MFH and an author of equestrian books. Her riding career began on a 'small, fat pony', which she rode with no saddle and using bits of string for reins, and with encouragement from Charlie, the family's Irish groom. When her parents moved to New York she progressed to lessons at the Gentlemen's Riding Club. 'Each Wednesday and Saturday I rode out with what was known as The Class: a dozen little girls like myself in sack coats and trim skirts with miniature bowlers on curls, together with as many little boys in tan whipcord.'

She soon began jumping (riding side saddle) at the major shows – The Garden, the Nassau Country Fair, Brooklyn, Rochester and Newport. At The Garden the hunters were expected to jump a row of six upright fences at about 5ft 4in, and when, at the age of eighteen, Lida was invited to show hunters at Olympia in 1913 (six years after this international show had first been organised by Lord Lonsdale), she was bitterly disappointed to discover that she would not be required to jump. By this time the Caprilli system of riding with a forward seat over fences was already becoming popular in Europe, but in America it was taking longer to be adopted. Lida Fleitmann had developed her own style of riding: 'In an era when Caprilli's theories were scarcely known in America, I nevertheless rode more forward in a side saddle than most of my contemporaries astride, adopting a position that, like the snaffle I always preferred, was not even considered at that epoch good form.'

Lida Fleitmann was a fearless rider to hounds, gaining a reputation for brave, and some-times reckless, riding across country. A great friend of hers, Tom Royden, wrote in a letter to her just before he died: 'I well remember my first day with the Meadow Brook . . . You knew me slightly in those days, or not at all, but I knew you, having been told in advance that if I could spare a neck or two it would be all right if I took you as a pilot.'

Her wanton nature took hold again when she bought a ticket to fly on the first civilian aeroplane to attempt a crossing of the Channel. The flight, from Le Bourget to Hounslow, took place shortly after the First World War in 'a storm so severe that it crippled steamship travel', according to a report in *The Times* the next day. 'Lt Shaw of Aircraft Transport and Travel Ltd piloted a plane from Paris to London in 1 hour and 55 minutes, with one passenger on board. The plane that should have made the voyage from London to Paris on the same day did not rise from the ground, for a torrential downpour of rain and a wind developing tornado proportions combined to make an attempt from the Hounslow aerodrome foolhardy.' According to Lida Fleitmann, 'We never reached our destination, Hounslow, pancaking into a ploughed field with a broken propeller. The rain was coming down in torrents, and, as the pilot climbed down from his seat, I saw coming across the muddy field a gentleman in tweeds. Aeroplanes dropping from the skies in those days were as rare as meteors, but this typical English gentleman neither asked us who we were, or where we came from, merely inquiring if we would like a cup of tea!'

When Lida Fleitmann visited London in 1913 to ride at Olympia, show jumping on the Continent had already become an established sport. Spain held its first international show at Barcelona in 1902, where one of the riders was Mme Rovira, who competed in the same events as her husband. The same year, another husband and wife partnership, Mr and Mrs Harry Buckland, represented Britian at the international show in Ostend. Another good rider was Mrs Philip Blackmore, who competed with some success at Olympia in the early days, and by the 1920s there were a number of good female riders taking part in this international show.

The appearance of Marjorie Bullows at Olympia in 1922 caused quite a stir, not only because she was an exceptional, if somewhat unorthodox, horsewoman, but also because she was the first woman to compete at the show riding astride. At a time when the idea of women riding in this way was still regarded as 'fast', Marjorie, a forthright and unconventional character, proved once and for all that women could ride astride just as well as men. She appeared at the show again in 1924, when she achieved the first clear round by a woman at Olympia on her 14.1hh pony If Not.

Marjorie Bullows (Lady Wright, after her marriage to Sir Robert Wright in 1928) was one of the most successful female show jumpers of her day. As a child she never had any riding lessons, but she was obviously a 'natural', and was determined to make her career with horses. She managed to start a small riding school business by coming to an arrangement with a cab and carriage owner in Moseley, just outside Birmingham, whereby she used the horses not in immediate work as school hacks, sharing the fees fifty-fifty with the owner. Eventually, when she came into some more money, she was able to buy her own riding stables at Metchely. Here she established the first school of its kind 'for training women in the art of Horsemanship and complete Stable Management, with a view to a career'. Marjorie Bullows had introduced the idea of 'working pupils'; among these was 'Pug' Verity, who, as Mrs Whitehead, was well known on the show-jumping circuit just after the Second World War, and Tinka Taylor, who rode Lady Wright's horses for twenty-two years and is now Chairman of the Junior Training Committee and the Junior International Committee.

If Not was bought by Marjorie in 1920. A liver chestnut gelding, he was said to have started his working life pulling a milk float, and was sent to her because he kept jumping out of his field; by 1928 his winnings had topped £3,000 at a time when first prize money, even at Olympia, was rarely more than £30. In 1927 Sir Robert bought his future wife a horse called Toby, with whom she won the Bath and West Championship and the Casani

Lady Wright (née Majorie Bullows) and Mistletoe winning at Richmond Horse Show. Lady Wright was the first woman to appear at Olympia riding astride.

Cup at Olympia – a high jump competition in which Toby cleared 7ft to beat horses from seven nations. A few years later, in 1936, Toby fell backwards after attempting to jump a wall, landing on Lady Wright and fracturing her pelvis, an injury from which she took many months to recover. But the following year, and just two weeks after fracturing her coccyx, she won the Daily Mail Cup and cleared 7ft 4in in the High Jump at Olympia, setting a new Ladies' record, with her most famous horse Jimmy Brown.

When show jumping had started up again on the Continent after the First World War its organisation was based mostly on private initiative, with the result that the competitions tended to be confined to the army and wealthy civilians. The rich and fashionable patronised the major international horse shows in an era that saw some outstanding women riders: Annelies Stoffel, wife of the Nations Cup rider Charley Stoffel, won the Puissance at the Geneva show in 1930 after clearing the wall at two metres; Irmgard von Opel from Germany became the first woman to win the famous Hamburg Derby in 1934. Another

Competitors at Lucerne in 1933: Mrs Stoffel, Mrs Haecky, Mrs Oppenheim, the Duchess of Morginano and Mrs Schwarzenbach.

sensational victory was achieved by Lilian Wittmack of Denmark when she won the Grand Prix of Lucerne in 1939, beating the *créme de la créme* of cavalry officers at that time.

The standard of the female jumpers was so high that major shows such as Lucerne and Aachen saw fit to host separate ladies' classes, and between 1929 and 1932 four (unofficial) Nations Cup competitions were held for lady riders. Germany had such a wealth of good female competitors during the 1930s that it asked the FEI (International Equestrian Federation) to consider holding a separate show jumping competition for women at the Olympic Games. The request was turned down, and it was not until 1956 that women show jumpers were first allowed to take part in the Olympics, when they rode on equal terms with the men.

By that time there had emerged in Britain one of the most outstanding show jumpers of all time, Pat Smythe. In her long and successful career she set up a phenomenal record: four times Ladies' European champion; European Ladies' High Jump record (set in Brussels in 1954 when she cleared 7ft 4½in riding Prince Hal); British National Champion a record eight times; a member of thirteen winning Nations Cup teams, and the first woman to win a team medal in Olympic show jumping. Born in East Sheen, on the outskirts of London, in 1928, she began riding at the age of three on a small pony called Bubbles. After Bubbles came Pixie, on whom Pat first began jumping – illicitly over the benches and fallen trees in Richmond Park. Her first attempt at leaving the ground was 'while the grown-ups were practising polo. I had a sudden impulse to try Pixie over some show jumps that had just been left in the corner of the field. Neither of us had jumped before, but Pixie in her astonishment leaped high in the air over the first fence at which I put her. I went flying, and the polo game was rudely interrupted by my yells of hurt pride.'[9] However, Pixie also gave Pat her first taste of success, when, in 1939, she jumped four clear rounds in the children's jumping class at the Richmond Horse Show to finish equal first.

Pat Smythe, aged $10\frac{1}{2}$, jumping Pixie at the Richmond Horse Show in 1939.

When Pat Smythe was sixteen her father died of an arthritic condition that had troubled him for many years. The family had to move from their home at Crickley, Gloucestershire, and take lodgings in Bath, where they rented a field for the ponies, and Pat's mother gave riding lessons to help with their keep. By this time they had already acquired the accident-prone mare Finality – the foal of a milk cart horse and a thoroughbred stallion – who was to bring Pat her first international successes. As a five-year-old, Finality nearly ripped off her hind legs on a barbed wire fence and the next year, following a bout of strangles, suffered another accident to one of her hind legs which put her out of action just before the Victory Jumping Competition at the White City; it was not until 1947 that she was able to make some impression as a possible international jumper. That was at the Bath and West Show, where she won two competitions, and finished second to Wilf White on Sharp Point in the final championship.

There then followed good performances at the International Horse Show – the first to be held since the war – bringing the pair to the attention of the selection committee. They were invited to make their debut for the British team in Ostend, where the team finished equal second, and Pat then went on to Le Zoute, where Finality was the only British horse to jump clear in the Grand Prix, in which they eventually finished fourth. She was only eighteen at the time. The following year this promising combination was separated when Finality was sold to Tommy Makin for the Irishman, Seamus Hayes, to ride. Pat Smythe had one of her last rides on the mare at the White City, where they qualified for the final of the King George V Gold Cup in the last year that women were allowed to compete in that event; a separate women's event, the Queen Elizabeth II Cup

– then the Princess's – was instituted in 1949. Given the chance to ride Finality once more at Haringey in 1949 she won the Leading Show Jumper of the Year class, and in the same year gained her first major international victory by winning the Grand Prix in Brussels with Mary Whitehead's Nobbler.

Pat Smythe had a remarkable ability to make successful show jumpers out of horses that other people had found unridable. That was how she came to own the grey mare Tosca, who was bought cheaply from Alan Oliver's yard because she was such a difficult ride. Another of her horses was Prince Hal, a broken down steeplechaser who Pat Smythe produced so well that he was borrowed for Olympic training in 1952. However, he never went to Helsinki; none of the men had succeeded in mastering his excitable temperament.

In 1956, when women were at last allowed to compete in the show jumping competition at the Olympic Games, Pat Smythe was selected for the British team in Stockholm, with Wilf White and Peter Robeson (in those days there were only three riders on each team). Riding Flanagan, the former event horse, she finished tenth out of sixty-six starters, helping the British team to secure the bronze medal.

The only other female show jumper at those Olympics was the Belgian rider Brigitte Schockaert, who finished in thirty-fourth place, but her team was eliminated. Brigitte, with her good horse, Muscadin, had won the Grand Prix of Lucerne just before the Games. At this same show Pat Smythe had won the Grand Prix Militaire, with the Italian, Giulia Serventi, second, but the winner of the cup is inscribed as Captain Bernard de Fombelle, who was in third place behind the two women – he was the best placed military rider! In May 1956, just before her performance in Stockholm, Pat Smythe was awarded the OBE. Four years later she and Flanagan again represented Britain at the Rome Olympics, where they put up another good performance to finish eleventh in the individual competition.

Since marrying the Swiss horse trials rider Sam Koechlin in 1963, Pat Koechlin-Smythe has spent much of her time living in Switzerland, though she has continued to maintain her ties with the sport in Britain, and for four years (1983–86) was President of the British Show Jumping Association. She is also a prolific author, with twenty-two books to her name. Probably the best known of these is her first book, *Jump for Joy*, an autobiography that was published before the historic Stockholm Olympics. It was an exceptionally well written book, illuminating and humorous, and it remains one of the best publications of its kind, despite the proliferation of equestrian 'life stories' that have since reached the bookstalls.

At the 1960 Olympics four British show jumpers had been selected to go to Rome, though only three were allowed to ride for the team. The fourth person had been Dawn Wofford (née Palethorpe) with Hollandia, a horse formerly ridden by her husband, War-ren. She had competed in the individual event, coming third in the first half, but a disastrous second round had left them in twentieth place. On the basis of that result, David Barker

(*left*) Pat Smythe riding Tosca in the *Country Life* and *Riding* Cup competition at the White City Stadium in 1953.

and Franco were put on the team, only to be eliminated after three refusals, the third being at the very last fence.

Dawn's international show jumping career had begun with a horse called Earlsrath Rambler, who had been produced by her sister, Jill, before her marriage to Peter Ward. Dawn took over the ride on Rambler in 1954, and the following year was selected to go with the British team to Paris and Germany. It was on this tour that Rambler and Dawn (then aged nineteen) firmly established their remarkable partnership. In Paris Rambler jumped a clear round in each of his classes, helping to make Dawn the leading lady rider; at the British Army Show in Germany, Rambler and Holywell Surprise (Dawn's second horse) between them won all but one of the international classes; and in Aachen Rambler won the ladies' class and the Puissance, as well as jumping two clear rounds in the Nations Cup, so that Dawn left the show with a new fur coat – her prize as the leading lady rider. On their return to England they went to the White City, where they won the *Country Life* Cup and the Queen Elizabeth II Cup – the first of two consecutive wins. Not surprisingly, the following year Dawn and her 15.2hh gelding (by then ten years old) went into training for the Olympic Games, but ultimately were only reserve for the team.

Dawn Palethorpe (now Mrs Wofford) with Earlsrath Rambler at Stockholm in 1956.

Following the Olympics, which took place in June, Britain won five Nations Cup competitions and Rambler was on the team on each occasion, jumping a total of eleven rounds in which he made only two mistakes. His other wins that year included the Queen Elizabeth II Cup and the Grand Prix of Rotterdam. Dawn's record for the 1956 season must have made the selectors regret leaving her off the Olympic team, but at that time Dawn was only twenty and was not as experienced as the other riders, and there was some doubt about Rambler's reliability at water jumps. 'I supported the selectors' decision wholeheartedly, but four years later, when I was given the wonderful chance of competing in the individual Olympic event at Rome, how I wished for Rambler at his best.'

By 1957 Rambler and Dawn were in demand at shows all over the world, and many invitations had to be turned down to avoid over-jumping her horse. That year he competed at Nice, Rome, Paris, the White City, Dublin, Rotterdam, Harrisburg, New York and Toronto, and seldom failed to bring home a trunk load of loot. In New York Dawn achieved her ambition of winning a class in Madison Square Garden, when she won the Drake Trophy.

Dawn and Warren Wofford were married after the American tour, and the following year, 1958, Dawn had her first child, Valerie. Within six weeks she was winning again at the Horse of the Year show on Hollandia. By then Hollandia was sixteen years old and only one of his lungs worked efficiently, so Dawn decided that he should not be put through the rigorous training given at the start of 1960 to the Olympic possibles. However, by the time the British team was due to go to Rome it was so short of sound horses that Dawn was asked to compete. Hollandia was not as well as he should have been for the individual competition, and a second round of jumping in the intense heat of the Rome arena proved too much to ask, resulting in a performance that lost Dawn her chance of riding for an Olympic team.

★   ★   ★

The Queen Elizabeth II Cup had been presented for the first time in 1949, giving women show jumpers their own championship in Britain. The first to win it, however, was an Irishwoman, Iris Kellet, one of the country's best female riders who has since become well known as a trainer. She triumphed again in 1951, and eighteen years later, at the age of forty-three, she became the oldest rider ever to win the Ladies' Individual European Championships, when the competition was held on her home ground of Dublin. Although there were only six competitors, she beat two of England's top riders of the day, Anneli Drummond-Hay (with the ex-eventer Merely-a-Monarch, on whom she had won the title the previous year), and Alison Westwood (The Maverick VII) to second and third places respectively.

The Ladies' Individual European Championship had been established in 1957, when it was held at Spa, Belgium. On that occasion Pat Smythe beat the Italian, Giulia Serventi, and the Frenchwoman, Michèle Cancre (now Madame d'Orgeix), to take the first Euro-

Iris Kellett on Short Lessons at the White City in 1963.

pean title. She won it again for three consecutive years from 1961 to 1963, setting a record that no one else surpassed. The ladies' competition merged with the men's in 1975, since when the individual European Championship has yet to be won by a female. It was not until 1952 that women were allowed to ride for Nations Cup teams, but when they did Michèle Cancre from France and Janine Mahieu from Belgium took the honours as the first ladies to represent their countries at the Nations Cup meeting in Rome. Later in the same year Pat Smythe rode for the winning British team at the White City, and by the 1953 Nations Cup competition in Rome there was a woman on every team – Natalie Perrone (on the winning Italian team), Helga Köhler (West Germany), Josée Bonnaud (France) and Pat Smythe for Britain.

By the early sixties the Americans were also producing some outstanding women riders, and at the 1964 Olympic Games in Tokyo two of their team were women – Kathy Kusner on Untouchable and Mary Mairs (later Mrs Chapot) on Tomboy joined forces with Frank Chapot on San Lucas. The team finished sixth. Britain did not field any women at that

(*above*) Competitors at the Ladies European Championships in 1960. From left to right: Bridget Schockaert (Belgium), Francois Vanderhaegen (Belgium), Giulia Serventi (Italy), Mme Zanuso (Italy), Anne Clement (Germany), Natalie Serventi (Italy), Dawn Wofford (GB), Susan Cohen (GB), ———?, Helga Kohler (Germany), Miss Lund (Denmark) and Miss Jansen (Holland).

(*left*) Olympic silver medallist, Marion Mould on Stroller, a bronze by Lorne McKean, and (*above*) after winning the *Country Life* and *Riding* Cup at the Horse of the Year Show in 1971.

Olympics, but Bridget McIntyre rode for Australia, and the Frenchwoman, Janou Lefèbvre, became the first woman to win an Olympic silver medal in show jumping when her team finished runners-up to West Germany.

The following year there came to the fore in Britain one of the most phenomenal partnerships in show jumping, when the 14.2hh Irish bred pony Stroller and his young rider Marion Coakes, fresh out of Junior competitions, won the first Ladies' World Championship and the Queen Elizabeth II Cup. Her outstanding performance that year, which also included three Nations Cup team successes, won her the Sportswoman of the Year award when she was only nineteen. In 1962 Marion and Stroller had been on the winning Junior European team in Berlin, where Stroller had jumped a double clear round, and in 1964 they won a team silver medal in the same championships in Budapest. When Marion graduated to senior competitions she persuaded her father to let her continue riding Stroller in them, even though he was so small; he was officially a pony, and was registered as such with the British Show Jumping Association. Within a year he had proved his ability to hold his own against the world's best horses, most of whom were at least six inches taller than him.

Remarkably for a horse of his size, Stroller excelled in the Hickstead Derby, jumping clear rounds on three occasions (more than any other horse in the history of the Derby), and winning there in 1967, when Marion was only twenty. The following year they were selected for the Mexico Olympics, where they put up a memorable performance, jumping one of only two clear rounds to win the individual silver medal – the first time a woman had won an individual Olympic medal in show jumping. By contrast, their performance in the team contest was a great disappointment and Stroller's elimination in the second round was put down to severe toothache, which had been troubling him throughout the Games. Within two years he was back on top form again, winning the 1970 Hamburg Derby with a clear round, the first to be ridden by a woman. The same year he was equal second in the Ladies' World Championship at Copenhagen, and won the Leading Show Jumper of the Year title at Wembley. He was retired the following year, but he lived to the grand age of thirty-six, dying on 24 March 1986.

Following Marion Coakes (now Mrs Mould) out of a successful junior show jumping career, Ann Moore won her first Ladies' European Championship in 1971 when she was twenty-one. She took the title again in 1973, the last year that separate events for men and women were held. Like Marion Mould, she won an individual Olympic silver medal – in Munich in 1972 – riding her brilliant horse, Psalm. She also won the Queen Elizabeth II Cup in the same year, and again in 1973 when she and Psalm tied with Alison Dawes and The Maverick.

Marion Coakes and Ann Moore had both been in their early twenties when they competed at the Olympic Games. In 1976 the Welsh girl, Debbie Johnsey, at nineteen, was the youngest competitor in the Olympic show jumping contest, as well as being the only woman. After two gruelling rounds over the big, solidly built course in Montreal, Debbie

Ann Moore on Psalm, on whom she won an individual Olympic silver medal in 1972.

Johnsey and Moxy had to negotiate the rain-soaked course once more in a three-way jump off for the silver and bronze medal positions. In that final round she was outjumped by Michel Vaillancourt (Canada) and Francois Mathey (Belgium), and so narrowly missed becoming the third consecutive British woman to win an individual Olympic medal.

Since Debbie Johnsey's brave performance in Montreal, up until 1988 no women have ridden for the British Olympic team, but at the 1984 Los Angeles there were two on the American team – Leslie Burr and Melanie Smith – who made history by becoming the first women to win an Olympic team gold medal in show jumping. Their victory in Los Angeles was indicative of the depth of talent among female show jumpers in America who, over the last ten years, have been more successful than those from any other country. Their dominance began to take hold as early as 1964, when Kathy Kusner and Mary Mairs represented the USA at the Tokyo Olympics. The same two women were on the US team again at the 1968 Mexico Olympics, and Kathy Kusner made her third consecutive Olympic appearance for the USA in Munich in 1972. No other woman has represented her country at three Olympic show jumping competitions. She was also the first woman to hold a licence as a professional flat jockey in the United States, and, at the age of thirty-one, was the first female to ride in the Maryland Cup – a race comparable to the Grand National at Aintree but run over timber fences.

Kathy Kusner riding Untouchable at Hickstead in 1967. This American rider made three consecutive Olympic appearances from 1964 to 1972.

In 1975 America's most outstanding woman rider, Melanie Smith, made her debut on a winning Nations Cup team in Washington, and although she was not selected for the 1976 Olympics, she took the individual bronze medal at the 'Alternative' Olympics at Rotterdam in 1980, when many of the Western countries boycotted the Moscow Games. Since her first international success in 1975, Melanie, who began riding at her parent's farm in Germantown, Tennessee, at the age of three, has been one of the most consistent riders on the show jumping circuit. In 1980, a year after the inauguration of the World Cup competition, she came second in the final to her compatriot Conrad Homfeld, and two years later won the contest in Gothenburg, thus becoming the first woman to win the World Cup Final. In doing so she beat the triple European champion Paul Schocke-mohle, who came second, as well as Hugo Simon and John Whitaker, who tied for third place. The following year, again riding Calypso, she was third in the World Cup, and then in 1984 won the team gold medal at the Olympics.

Leslie Burr, the other woman on that successful Los Angeles team, won the World Cup Final in 1976 on a horse called McLain. The following year, 1977, the title was won by yet another American woman, Katharine Burdsall, while Lisa Jacquin, also from the USA, finished third behind France's Philippe Rozier. Just to rub in their supremacy, in 1986 an all-woman American team (Anne Kursinski, Katharine Burdsall, Lisa Tarnapol

Leslie Burr (USA) at the 1984 Olympics.

and Katie Monahan) won the Nations Cup in Washington, and the following year, at Hickstead, repeated the exercise with another all-women team, this time comprising Deborah Dolan, Joan Scharffenberger, Anne Kursinski and Katie Monahan. No other country has produced so many top class women show jumpers in recent years; Britain comes next in line.

★   ★   ★

From the second half of the 1960s and throughout the 1970s one woman in particular was reaping the rewards of her dedication to the sport: her name was Caroline Bradley. From an international debut in 1966, when she was twenty, she maintained her position as one of the key riders on the British team for seventeen years. She represented Britain on twelve winning Nations Cup teams, and was a member of the gold medal teams at the 1978 World Championships and the 1979 European Championships. In 1983, at the age of thirty-seven, she died of heart failure.

Her death stunned the show jumping world. A tribute in *The Times* read: 'Without doubt she was far and away the most outstanding woman rider of show jumpers in the world. She kept her own counsel, and her qualities of character brought a unique distinction and dignity to show jumping. She was the pattern for young aspirants and she will be quite irreplaceable.' Stress and overwork were almost certainly the main cause of this tragedy. In her determination to get back to the top of the sport after the loss of her brilliant horse Tigre, Caroline drove herself to the limit; she worked night and day, regularly rode eight or nine horses at a show, spent hours at the wheel of her horsebox, and always strove to maintain the exceptionally high standards that she had set herself.

From an early age Caroline had shown an extraordinary patience in training horses. Even as a schoolgirl, 'Getting the best from an animal became something of an obsession with her', according to Malcolm Severs, who wrote a book about her shortly after she died. A natural understanding of horses combined with a highly competitive spirit were the forces behind her success, yet she was also a shy, modest person, with no desire to be a prima donna. Once she had chosen to make her career in horses, Caroline's parents gave her all the support they could, both financially and morally, and it was not long before they were rewarded for their faith in their daughter. After eighteen months of gruelling training with Lars Sederholm at Waterstock, Caroline was selected to ride at Dublin Horse Show – her first international show – where she won two classes. The following year, at the age of twenty-one, she firmly established herself on the international circuit by winning the Civilian Open Championship at Toronto, and then coming second to Harvey Smith in the New York Grand Prix.

Although she continued to ride for the British team at international competitions (and, incidentally, competed at the Badminton Horse Trials in 1969 on Lars Sederholm's Alpaca, finishing sixteenth), Caroline was not selected for the 1972 Olympics, and instead set her sights on the 1976 Games. But in 1973, following a decision by the FEI to straighten out

(*above*) Debbie Johnsey riding Moxy at the Montreal Olympics where she narrowly missed an individual medal.

(*below*) Junior European Champion, Gillian Greenwood.

HRH Princess Anne competing on Saint John at Aldon in 1986.

the anomalies in the classification of amateur and professional show jumpers, Caroline was forced to turn professional. She appealed against the decision on the basis that, although she rode horses for other people, she was not paid to do so, but the British Show Jumping Association would not rescind its decision. Ironically, in 1987, four years after her death, those show jumpers who had been forced to turn professional were allowed to reclassify their status and compete in the Olympics.

In 1974 Caroline created history when she became the first woman to win the Puissance at the Horse of the Year Show, Wembley, and the following year had an outstanding victory in the Hamburg Derby, coming first with New Yorker and second with Acrobat. By now she had already begun to establish her famous partnership with John Harding's stallion Marius, on whom she won the Queen Elizabeth II Cup in 1978, and in 1977 she began riding the big grey gelding Tigre. It was with this horse that Caroline was to achieve her greatest successes.

The late Caroline Bradley and Tigre. Caroline died of heart failure in 1983.

The men's and women's world championships were amalgamated for the first time in 1978, and were held in Aachen, Germany. Caroline was the only woman to take part in these championships. Riding Tigre, she had a disappointing performance in the preliminary speed competition – three fences down and time faults – but the next day produced two superb clear rounds, the best performance by a British rider, to secure the gold medal for her team. In the subsequent Grand Prix competition, in which the leading four riders change horses to contest the individual world champion title, she missed qualifying for the jump off by just one quarter of a time fault.

The next two years saw Caroline at her pinnacle. Riding Tigre, she won a gold medal with the British team at the 1979 European Championships, was leading rider at the Royal International Horse Show, won the President's Cup in Calgary, and won World Cup qualifiers at Birmingham and Dublin. The following year she won the Grand Prix at Hickstead, took the Queen Elizabeth II Cup for the second time, topped the money winners' list and was elected Sportswoman of the Year.

Then came the greatest blow to Caroline's career: the owner of Tigre, Donald Bannocks, decided to put the horse up for sale. At first it looked as if there would be a reprieve for Caroline when she agreed to sell her half share of Tigre, and she was subsequently allowed to keep her ride on the horse. But when, early in 1981, Caroline signed a sponsorship deal with the oil company Tricentrol, Mr Bannocks sent a horsebox to Caroline's yard to take Tigre away. It was a tremendous set-back: not only had Caroline lost her best horse, but she had nothing in her stables to replace him. She would have to start all over again with youngsters. The disappointment, coupled with the urgent need to produce more top class horses and achieve good results for her new sponsors, put Caroline under tremendous pressure. She worked tirelessly, putting in even longer hours. 'There can be no doubt that it was her dedication, her refusal to compromise, her contemptuous disregard for her own pain and her single-minded determination to get back to the very top that eventually killed her', wrote Malcolm Severs. In June 1983, at the Suffolk Show, Ipswich, Caroline collapsed after competing in the main class. She died on the way to hospital.

The only other woman rider in Britain who had been a serious rival to Caroline was Liz Edgar. Though three years Caroline's senior, Liz's greatest successes began in the late 1970s, following the birth of her only child, Maria, in 1971. Since then she has been a regular member of the British team in Nation Cup competitions, has won the Queen Elizabeth II Cup an unprecedented five times, and has been ranked among the top ten riders in this country for the last twelve years.

The Edgars were among the first show jumpers in Britain to take on sponsorship when they signed up with Everest Double Glazing in 1970, and Liz has been riding horses under their banner ever since. On Everest Maybe she won the Ladies' National Championship at Windsor in 1975 and 1977 – the year that she gained the first of her Queen Elizabeth II Cup victories and also won the Grand Prix of New York at Madison Square Garden, becoming the first British woman to take this award. Three years later she became the first woman ever to win the Aachen Grand Prix.

With a background that was unlikely to lead her to any other career, Liz began jumping in pony classes as a young child, going round the shows with her father, Fred Broome, and elder brother David. At the age of twelve she made her first appearance at the Horse of the Year Show on a 13.2hh pony called Nutshell, and at sixteen won three pony championships – the Royal Show, the Three Counties and the Royal Welsh. Her first taste of international competition came in 1960 when she rode for the winning British team at the Junior European Championships in Venice, Italy. The only other girl on the team was Jane Kidd, who was later to make a name for herself in dressage. Three years later Liz was invited to ride for the senior team in Ostend and Rotterdam, and at the latter venue jumped two clear rounds in the Nations Cup and came second in the Grand Prix.

In spite of this highly satisfactory first venture at senior international level, Liz lacked the confidence to ride in the 1964 Olympics, opting instead to lend her top horse, Jacapo, to her brother David to take to Tokyo. 'I just didn't feel that I was ready for that sort of class,' says Liz who, since then, has not had the opportunity to ride for an Olympic team. Self-effacement was also one of Caroline Bradley's characteristics, and both these women had to overcome a natural diffidence to compete at international level.

American women, perhaps as a result of the training and back-up they receive from the USET (United States Equestrian Team) and better financial assistance, seem to handle the international competitions with more assurance. 'The rich people in America are prepared to buy the best horses for the girls to ride,' says Liz Edgar, who regards British riders as the poor relations to the Americans when it comes to buying horses. Nevertheless, show jumping in the USA is still a relatively low-profile sport, and in 1987, when Lisa Tarnapol signed an agreement with Revlon, she was the first female American show jumper to take on commercial sponsorship.

In Britain more women chose to make their career in eventing than show jumping, partly because the financial pressures of the latter are so great. 'Top horses for show jumping are very few and far between, and they are worth so much money. You could struggle all your life, but if you haven't got a special horse to take you show jumping you can forget it.' Liz Edgar also thinks that more girls are attracted to eventing because they can be reasonably successful on an averagely talented horse, without having to spend thousands of pounds. They also have outstanding examples to which they can aspire. 'Ginny Leng is the most wonderful ambassador for eventing. Her approach and outlook must effect young girls growing up. They want to be like her. I remember when I was a kid I wanted to be like Pat Smythe.'

Nevertheless there are talented women show jumpers coming to the fore in Britain, some of them from Liz Edgar's own yard. Liz and her husband Ted have been responsible for nurturing a number of good, female riders – Lesley McNaught (the 1981 Junior European Champion and Ladies' Champion), Janet Hunter and Emma Jane Mac. Now they have their own daughter, Maria, on whom to concentrate, and she has already shown flair in senior competitions. In a few years time Liz may well be content to sit back and let her daughter take the limelight.

In the meantime, one of the most serious challenges to Liz Edgar's position as Britain's leading lady show jumper comes from Gillian Greenwood who, in 1987, at the age of twenty, won the Queen Elizabeth II Cup at the Royal International Horse Show. Her

Janet Hunter on Everest
Lisnamarrow, winner of the 1988
Queen Elizabeth II Cup.

Gail Greenough (Canada), the
first woman to win the World
Championships.

victory was the essence of good timing, for she was on the verge of losing her best horse, Monsanta, after a six-figure offer had been made for the gelding by an overseas rider at the show. Her father, former international rider John Greenwood, was not in a strong enough position financially to ignore an offer of that kind, and the horse would almost certainly have been sold if a sponsor had not come forward. Fortunately, the Director of Landsaver MCP was at the show when Gillian achieved her victory in the Queen Elizabeth II Cup, and, hearing of her plight, stepped in with a sponsorship deal to support both Gillian and her younger sister, Julie.

Gillian's first major international success was in 1984 when she won the individual gold medal at the Junior European Championships in Belgium. She was riding Sky Fly, an ex-hurdler who had broken down while show jumping with Gillian's father. After two years off work, the mare was taken back into competition by Gillian, and has been successful at junior and senior level. Her top horse, Monsanta, came from Ireland in 1985. Since teaming up with him Gillian has had numerous wins – the Grand Prix in Salzburg, the Queen Elizabeth II Cup, the Silk Cut Trophy at Hickstead and the team and individual gold medals at the European Young Rider's Championships in 1987. Gillian's performance at these championships was outstanding. She jumped two clear rounds in the Nations Cup, enabling her team to overtake the French for the lead position, and in the individual contest achieved the only double clear to win a second gold medal.

One woman whose name will be forever engraved in the history books of show jumping is Gail Greenough. From being almost unknown on the international circuit, the 26-year-old Canadian shot to fame in 1986 when, against all apparent odds, she won the World Championships in Aachen. She was competing on the German-bred Mr T, a horse that was ridden as a novice by the late Caroline Bradley, but in the four-horse jump off had to ride the other qualifiers as well – Nick Skelton's Apollo, Pierre Durand's Jappeloup de Luze and Conrad Homfeld's Abdullah. Against these three experienced riders Gail's chances looked bleak, yet she was the only one to jump all four horses clear. Since the first individual World Championships open to both men and women were held in 1978, no woman has competed in the final jump off, let alone won the gold medal. It was a remarkable achievement for someone who had her first riding lessons at the age of eleven, and who was making only her second appearance in Europe. Gail's advantage lay in her sympathetic handling of the strange horses that she had to ride at Aachen, and her own ability to form a good relationship with the temperamental Mr T. She had been his only rider for three years before the World Championships, and his response to unknown, male jockeys was to tense up and become headstrong. Both Pierre Durand and Nick Skelton had disastrous rounds with him, and only Conrad Homfeld jumped him clear.

In the 1978 World Championships Caroline Bradley had been the only female rider. In 1982 in Dublin there had been two women, and in 1986 there were seven out of a field of seventy-two. Women, particularly those in Europe, are still lagging seriously behind the men in quantity if not quality.

CHAPTER FOUR
EVENTING

Over the last two decades eventing has increasingly become the domain of women, particularly in Britain. At the 1975 and 1983 European Championships Britain put forward all-female teams, which on both occasions won the silver medal, and, since 1973, both Badminton and Burghley have been won more times by women than men. On the Continent the 'Amazones' have not fared as well, though they are on the increase, while in America, Australia and New Zealand there are a growing number of good female competitors in this sport.

Considering that it was not until 1964 that women were first allowed to compete in three-day events at Olympic level, their success has been phenomenal. There was just one female event rider at the 1964 Games; twenty years later there were eighteen women competing out of forty-eight competitors at the three-day event in Los Angeles. The growing predominance of women in Britain is due largely to the present structure of the sport. To reach the top these days it is necessary to be dedicated to the task, yet the prize money is not high enough to compensate financially for the many hours of work that have to be spent training a horse to its peak of fitness and ability. Although the more successful riders can usually obtain some form of sponsorship, it is by no means guaranteed, and few men are prepared to give up other responsibilities to devote all their time to a sport that offers such a precarious means of living. Women, on the other hand, are often in the enviable position of having fewer financial obligations, particularly if they do not have a family. Nevertheless, there are many who have had to overcome considerable hardships to partake in the sport, and who have succeeded in turning it into a rewarding career.

Of the three Olympic equestrian disciplines, eventing took the longest to open its doors to women for two main reasons. The first lay in the sport's origins: horse trials had been introduced as a test of endurance for military horses, and the earliest competitions, even at Olympic level, were confined to serving army officers. The second reason was simply that the arduous and sometimes dangerous nature of the sport caused the Olympic Committee to baulk at the idea of female participation. It was only because the British women, by their consistent success both at home and abroad, proved again and again that they were capable of holding their own in this demanding sport, that the authorities finally relented and agreed to their inclusion at Olympic level.

Although Britain had sent riders to the 1912 and subsequent Olympics, their best result had been a team bronze at the 1936 Berlin Games, and there was little interest in the sport in England until well after the Second World War. A few 'combined training' competitions (dressage and jumping) had been established, and in 1946 one of these competitions also included a cross country course, thus making it the first one-day event to be run under a similar format to modern day horse trials. It was won by a woman.

The competition was organised at Wellesbourne by Lt Col R. V. F. Brackenbury, who had made up the dressage test himself. It seems that his ideas were slightly over-ambitious, for the test concluded with three flying changes on a straight line – a movement that was well beyond the capabilities of most of the competitors. There then followed a cross country course over natural fences (misprinted in the programme as 'national' fences), after which riders went straight into the ring and completed the show jumping course. Lorna Johnstone, who ten years later became one of the first dressage riders to represent Britain at the Olympics, won the competition on her versatile horse Greatheart.

Following a disastrous performance by the British at the 1948 Olympic three-day event at Aldershot, where the team was eliminated and Peter Borwick, who finished seventeenth, was the best-placed British rider, the Duke of Beaufort felt moved to do something about it. 'It was when I stood at Aldershot watching the efforts of our team with a deepening sense of gloom, that the germ of an idea came to my mind,' he wrote in his memoirs. The idea was to hold a competition, along the lines of the Olympic Horse Trials, in the park at Badminton each year, so that British horses and riders would be provided with the necessary encouragement and experience to compete at international level. The 'Great Event' was an immediate success, and within five years the British teams began to reap the benefit of these new trials, winning the 1953, 1954 and 1955 European Championships, and the 1956 Olympic Games.

Since its inauguration in 1949, Badminton has fielded female winners on 15 occasions. In the very first event five women took part – a high proportion considering that out of the twenty-two starters twelve were from the services. In other words, half of the civilian riders were women. Only thirteen horses completed the three days, but among them was Vivien Machin Goodall's Neptune, who finished fifth. None of the other four women who had taken part – Elaine Knox-Thompson, who ran a riding school near Towcester, with her mare Salome; Pat Oliver on Mrs J. James Pearce's Golden Archer; Susan Poile, of show jumping fame, on Freddie, and Biddy Clowes on Brigadier Martin's Black Boy – completed the event, so Vivien Machin Goodall (later Mrs Boon) became the first women to negotiate Badminton successfully. Vivien competed again on Neptune at Badminton

Penelope Molteno on Carmena at Badminton in 1953.

in 1950, finishing fifteenth, and in 1953, when they came fifth, and Vivien was awarded the special prize given by the Duke of Beaufort for the best girl rider at Badminton that year. The following autumn they won the inaugural three-day event at Harewood, where, together with Penelope Molteno who came second, they beat such names as Laurence Rook on Starlight, Brigadier Bolton on Flanagan (a horse later show jumped by Pat Smythe) and Frank Weldon on Kilbarry. In the same year Vivien and Neptune also competed in show jumping classes at the White City and Haringey.

Vivien's performance at the first Badminton had not gone unnoticed; Brigadier F. E. Bowden Smith wrote that Neptune had been 'ridden by Miss Machin Goodall with calm and determination . . . this horse is a great jumper. He cleared twenty-two feet at the water jump without effort and finished as fresh as a daisy. If his dressage can be improved Neptune is a future Olympic horse.' But there was the nub of it. Even if Neptune had been regarded as a possible Olympic mount, Vivien would not have been allowed to ride him. It was the same story throughout the next fourteen years: British girls were producing outstanding horses which they were then expected to hand over to men to ride for the Olympic teams. It was a problem that caused much anguish and hard feeling among riders, owners and the Selection Committee. One of the people to be caught up in the Olympic dilemma was Margaret Hough, who, in 1954 became the first woman to win Badminton. She began

Margaret Hough on Bambi at the water jump at Badminton in 1954, the year she became the first woman to win this event.

eventing in 1952 with an Irish-bred mare called Bambi V, and succeeded in being placed third when attempting her first one-day event at Gisburne Park, Yorkshire. Her performance had been spotted by Tony Collings, who had become official coach to the British team (sadly, he was killed two years later in a Comet air disaster over the Mediterranean), and he asked Margaret if she would consider lending her horse to the British Olympic Team.

Hylton Cleaver, who had written his book *They've Won Their Spurs* to highlight the injustice of excluding women event riders from the Olympic Games, was of the view that the policy of borrowing horses was one that did not always do the team, or the horse, much good. When Margaret Hough agreed to lend Bambi for the Helsinki Olympics she 'lost the horse for eight months, and when it came back it hardly knew her . . . Although Bambi had been looked after at Porlock by Wendy Jones, handling by men had changed her nature, and it took quite a while to bring her back to her old form. Just as this had been achieved, Margaret was asked to lend Bambi again to the British team for Badminton for 1953. She sighed and agreed, because Bertie Hill was to ride, but they did not really get on together, and came rather far down the list.'

When Bambi was selected for the 1952 Games Margaret made the stipulation that she must go with her to Helsinki as groom. It turned out that all the grooms who accompanied the British horses to the Olympics were girls – Joyce Whittaker, Madeline Weeks, Wendy

Jones, June Le-Tall and Josephine Garratt. According to Hylton Cleaver the girl grooms won 'the admiration of all others who were in Finland for the condition of the British horses' and for their 'quiet, steady industry'. Brigadier Peatt had apparently written home to say that, being the only girl grooms at the Games, they had caused a sensation, and that the male grooms of other countries were falling over themselves in their efforts to help. 'One morning,' he wrote, 'as I arrived at the stables, Wendy appeared pushing an enormous wheelbarrow full of manure. The cynosure of all eyes, she attempted to run up a ramp into a truck and got stuck half way. Immediately there was a mad rush of soldiers to help, which caused her to subside on the ground in helpless laughter.'

In the end Bambi did not compete at Helsinki because she developed a rash under her girth, and instead Bertie Hill rode Stella, a horse lent to the team by Major John Miller. However, the British team were eliminated when Major Laurence Rook, concussed from a fall, went the wrong side of the flag at the finish of the cross country. When, in 1954, Margaret Hough had the opportunity to compete again on her own horse, she made history by becoming the first woman to win Badminton. It was the year for women riders, for Diana Mason came third at the same event on her diminutive bay mare Tramella, and both women were subsequently selected to represent Britain at the European Championships at Basle.

Although Margaret Hough competed in Basle, she was left out of the team because Bambi was suspected of having a 'stop', so Diana Mason became the first woman to ride for a British team at an international championships. The two British women were the only female competitors at Basle, and they put up outstanding performances to finish sixth and seventh respectively in what was regarded as the toughest international event since the Berlin Olympics. Lt Col C. E. G. Hope takes up the story: 'The speed and endurance phase was of Olympic length – twenty-two miles – over an exceedingly hilly terrain; nearly every fence was on a slope, to be met either up or down; the obstacles were nearly of the maximum allowed, and uphill approaches to many of them made them actually five feet and more. One indeed was lowered after protests by all the teams.

'There was one obstacle, the "river crossing", which nearly wrecked the whole competition. The "river" was a running stream, about 3ft deep, with an uneven bottom and steep, slippery 3ft banks on either side. There had been a lot of rain in the preceding days, and the clay soil was heavy and glutinous, with all the resilience of treacle.'[10] The obstacle became impassable quite early on, causing the elmination of two Swedish horses, and it was clear that unless it was modified it would throw the competition into jeopardy.

After lengthy discussions it was agreed that the obstacle would be altered and the two Swedish horses reinstated. Margaret Hough was actually approaching the river while the organisers were considering their dilemma, and had to be warned by one of the British committee to ease up and find out what she was expected to do. Diana Mason's Tramella, only 15hh, had to swim across the river, and later had a fall at fence 27, but still completed the course – a commendable feat in itself considering eleven of the twenty-eight starters were eliminated and two more had to be withdrawn the following morning. No-one achieved a clear round on the cross country, but the event was still a walkover for the British riders. Their team won the gold medal, and Britain came away with all the individual medals as well. What is more, the two British girls had beaten all but two of their foreign rivals and proved themselves to be every bit as competent as the men at international championship level.

Diana Mason and Tramella at Badminton in 1954, when they came third. Diana Mason subsequently became the first woman to ride for a team at an international three-day event.

The following year Diana Mason rode again for the British team at the European Championships at Windsor, where, as in Basle, she took the lead after the dressage phase. But Tramella slipped and fell after landing from a fence on the cross country. The fall, the first Tramella had ever had, clearly upset her, and she refused to jump the next fence. Tramella never really regained her enthusiasm for eventing after this fall, and Diana decided to turn her attention to dressage. A visit to the equestrian Olympics in Stockholm in 1956 had given her a taste of dressage. 'It was the first time I had ever seen a grand prix test, and I was so impressed I decided that I would like to try it.' Tramella, only ten years old when she stopped eventing, had already had an interesting career. She was bought by Diana as a four-year-old to be shown as a hack and small working hunter, at which she had considerable success. A pretty bay mare with four white socks, she was by the premium stallion Tramail out of a Welsh Pony mare. Soon after arriving at the Mason's Warwickshire home she demonstrated her jumping talents by leaping over a gate and cutting her leg so badly that she was off work for six weeks.

As a five-year-old Tramella competed in her first one-day events, and made headlines by winning the trials at Epperstone in Nottinghamshire where she beat John Oram, one of the Olympic short-listed riders. But she was not an easy horse to ride for she had a hot temperament – at Basle she had to be ridden for five hours before her dressage test. Yet after her retirement from horse trials she became equally successful at dressage, and subsequently became the only horse ever to have been on a winning European Championship team in both eventing and dressage (the latter being at the 1963 Copenhagen championships, when the British team scored their only victory in international dressage, largely due to the fact that so many of the other competitors had had to withdraw through illness or lameness). She was retired from dressage at the age of eighteen.

★   ★   ★

If women had been allowed to compete in Olympic three-day events in the 1950s one person who almost certainly would have ridden for the British team was Sheila Willcox. For three consecutive years between 1957 and 1959 she won the Badminton Horse Trials – a record that has yet to be surpassed – and in 1957 became the first woman to win a European Championship when she took both the team and individual gold medals in Copenhagen. It was tragic that her outstanding eventing career did not include an Olympic performance, at first because women were not allowed on the team, and later, in 1968, because she narrowly missed selection – a decision which caused a good deal of hard feeling at the time. Sheila began riding as a small child when her mother bought her a Dartmoor pony called Folly – an appropriate name as it turned out, for when the pony arrived they discovered it was unbroken. After Folly came a show pony called Sweet Sue and another pony called Sheriff, with whom Sheila had great success in 13.2hh show jumping classes. She graduated to a 14.2hh show pony, Ecstasy, and another jumper called Gentleman Jim, before riding her first horse, Blithe Spirit, who she produced as a show hack. When she was seventeen, her father bought High and Mighty. Both horse and rider were novices at eventing, but within eighteen months were competing in their first three day event.

Sheila set the seal on her eventing career by winning her first one-day trial – at Hovingham in Yorkshire – and followed this up with another victory at Tetbury. The next season, 1955, they competed at Glenusk and Stowell Park, before tackling the Windsor three-day event, which that year had taken on European Championship status. As a newcomer, she impressed the selectors by finishing thirteenth in a strong field that included five international teams, and when she came fourth at Harwood later in the year she was invited to train for the team that was to go to the international event in Turin. It was

Sheila's first event abroad; she was nineteen and the only woman in the competition in Turin. She won the event, beating Germany's leading horse trials rider, August Lütke-Westhues, and riders from five other countries. It was a meteoric rise to fame, but no fluke. She maintained a consistently good eventing record on High and Mighty and on her next horse Airs and Graces, and then made something of a comeback to eventing in 1964 with Glenamoy, before winning Burghley with Fair and Square in 1968.

Sheila Willcox with High and Mighty at Badminton in 1957, when she achieved the first of her three consecutive wins.

After Sheila's performance in Turin, the selectors, not surprisingly, looked to High and Mighty when it came to the 1956 Olympics. Again, here was a potential Olympic horse ridden by a woman. At first it looked as if the selectors would have no need to call upon High and Mighty, but as various horses went lame or proved unsuitable, they found that they were left with just Kilbarry (Frank Weldon) and Countryman (Bertie Hill) as certainties. The pressure on Sheila to lend her horse to the Olympic team became considerable. Lt Col C. E. G. Hope explains what happened: Sheila 'had already refused a good offer for the horse in Italy and knew full well, what the selectors seemed to have overlooked, that it was the combination which counted, especially when the human partner was a girl. However, the selectors, mistakenly as it proved to be, were determined to get hold of High and Mighty, resorting even to Royal intervention, and finally the impasse was resolved by Mr Marsh buying High and Mighty himself – promising that Sheila would have the ride of him next year – and handing him over together with his promising newcomer, Wild Venture, to the British team . . . in the end High and Mighty never went to Stockholm. Not unexpectedly he and Michael Naylor-Leyland did not get on together, and he went lame in training, so all the fuss and anxiety were wasted.'

The British team still managed to win the gold medal in Stockholm, and Frank Weldon took the individual bronze medal. The following year Sheila got her horse back and gained the first of three consecutive Badminton wins. By this time American women were also beginning to make their mark on the eventing world, and in 1958 at the National three-day event for the John W. Wofford Memorial Trophy at Colorado Springs women finished second, third and fourth. It was certainly an encouraging result for the women – Mrs Davis on Gipsy Hill, Camille Stahl on Miss Butch and Mrs Rolofson on Echuca Boy – but since the winner of the event, Jonas Irbinskas, was a professional and women were still barred from the Olympics, it left the American team selectors in a quandary.

The same problem hit the British selectors at the 1960 Badminton, when the Australians Bill Roycroft and Larrie Morgan filled the first two places, and Anneli Drummond-Hay with Perhaps, who had led all the way until faulting in the show jumping, came third. Once again the best British performance had to be disregarded because women were not allowed to compete in the Olympics. Two years later Anneli Drummond-Hay succeeded in winning Badminton with Merely-A-Monarch, on whom she had won the inaugural three-day event at Burghley in 1961; but she then switched this brilliant horse to show jumping, so that she could at least have a chance of representing Britain at the Olympics, since women had been included in the show jumping team since 1956. Merely-A-Monarch made the transition without difficulty, competing on two winning Nations Cup teams in 1963. In 1968, following a period of physical problems, he helped Anneli to win the Ladies' European Championships, and in 1970 won the Queen Elizabeth II Cup at the Royal International Horse Show.

It is ironic that when, in 1964, women at last got their chance to compete at an Olympic three-day event, no British women were selected for the team. Susan Fleet and Sheila Willcox had been the two most likely contenders for a place, but in the spring of that year Susan Fleet's horse The Gladiator broke down at Badminton, and at the final trial at Burghley in the autumn Sheila Willcox and Glenamoy (winners of Little Badminton that year) had a refusal at Capability's Cutting and a fall at the Trout Hatchery. So when the team for Tokyo was chosen no women were included, and it was left to an American rider, Helen du Pont, to become the first woman to take part in an Olympic three-day event. As Hope wrote: 'It was a little hard on the British girls, who had pioneered female participation in this sport ever since the war, to have been robbed of this distinction.' Helen du Pont had competed in England with her Olympic horse, Mr Wister, in previous years with moderate success, and in Tokyo she finished thirty-third in the final reckoning after two heavy falls on the cross country.

Three years later, Burghley Horse Trials saw the launching of one of the sport's most consistent and talented riders when, at the age of twenty-three, Lorna Sutherland (now

Lorna Sutherland (now Mrs Clarke) jumping into the Lake at Badminton on Popadom. In 1970 she became the first (and only) woman to ride three horses round the Badminton cross country in one day.

The first woman to win an Olympic team gold medal in eventing: Jane Bullen (now Mrs Holderness-Roddam) on Our Nobby, after completing their dressage test in Mexico in 1968.

Mrs Clarke) won the event on her 'skewbald pony club runner' Popadom. Showing the determination that has been the hallmark of her riding ever since, she persuaded Popadom to gallop round the steeplechase course with sixteen seconds to spare after friends had commented that it was a pity that the little 'cob' would not be fast enough. It had already surprised people that Popadom had managed to achieve the top dressage score of the event. Hope's comments were quite scathing: 'The event was notable for the success of Lorna Sutherland, who won decisively with Popadom, thanks to the generosity of the judges who awarded this excellent but plodding horse no less than 80.33% (equivalent to 28 penalties) dressage marks, which put him in the category of Durlas Eile at Punchestown and other past performers, which was manifestly absurd.'

Lorna was also riding a horse called Nicholas Nickleby, and had she not taken the wrong course in the show jumping, she would have finished third on him. Three years later she made history by becoming the only woman to ride three horses round Badminton, and has since been included on numerous British teams, including the 1983 and 1985 European Championships and the 1986 World Championships, where she won the team gold and individual bronze medals. Twenty-one years after that first victory at Burghley, Lorna is still competing with success in the top events.

In 1968 the first British woman took part in the Olympic three-day event. Her name was Jane Bullen, and she had clinched her place on the team by winning at Badminton that spring on a small horse called Our Nobby. At the time Jane, who was nineteen, was working as a nurse at the Middlesex hospital, and her elder sister Jennie (Loriston Clarke) had been helping look after her horse and get him fit. Our Nobby was a remarkable horse. He arrived on the Bullen's doorstep one day with a local farmer who was keen to sell him. Jane's mother agreed to the purchase, intending to school him and then sell him on, but he turned out to be so nappy that they had little option but to keep him. Jane can recall several battles with him, the most vivid being at the Craven hunter trials, where, following yet another elimination, she and her mother decided it was time to sort out his obstinate ways once and for all. When the event had finished they went back to the obstacle in question – a coffin – and duly tried to persuade Our Nobby to jump it. 'We were there until 10 p.m. using the car lights to see our way. Eventually he gave in.'

That was the turning point, and, by 1967, when Our Nobby was twelve years old, he was proficient enough to tackle his first Badminton, though he nearly failed to qualify on the grounds of his size. He was just 15hh, the minimum height for a senior international three-day event. That year he and Jane finished fifth, and the following year, after a typically appalling dressage test which had put them in twenty-ninth place, this nippy little horse scorched round the cross country (he was the only horse to finish within the optimum time) to take Jane into second place. When Sgt Ben Jones and Foxdor knocked a fence down in the show jumping the following day, 'The Galloping Nurse', as she was later to be dubbed by the popular press, won her first Badminton.

Although Sheila Willcox won the final Olympic trial at Burghley that autumn with

Karen Stives riding Ben Arthur at the 1984 Olympics, where she won the team gold and individual silver medals in the three-day event.

Lucinda Green and Mins Lincoln on their way to winning the 1987 Chatsworth three-day event.

The 1986 World Dressage Champion: Anne Grethe-Jensen (Denmark) on Marzog.

Fair and Square, she was not included in the team for Mexico, the selectors naming her as reserve. Sheila then set off a storm of protest by refusing to travel to Mexico on the grounds that she did not want to risk the horse unnecessarily on such a long journey. She had her sympathisers, for many people felt that her performance at Burghley merited her inclusion on the team, and that this would have given her the Olympic recognition which the rules of ten years ago had denied her.

In the end Jane Bullen was the only female British event rider to travel to Mexico, though there were three women on the Irish team – Juliet Jobling Purser, Diana Willson and Penny Moreton, one of Ireland's top event riders. No other women competed in the three-day event, and of those four only one failed to finish the competition – a reasonable result considering there were forty-four falls on the cross country. The riders had to cope with appalling conditions. The cross country was still being built as the competitors arrived in Mexico, which meant that the ground on either side of the fences had not had

Early days: Jennie (holding pony) and Jane Bullen.

time to settle, a problem that was aggravated by the weather: in the mornings the heat baked the top soil into a hard layer, and in the afternoons the monsoon-type rainstorms made it wet and slippery. At the takeoff and landing of each fence the horses' feet went straight through the top layer into soft ground underneath. 'It was a horrible feeling,' says Jane. 'The ground gave way as the horses took off.'

The water jumps were the worst affected. At the second of these (there were four altogether) there were twenty-two falls, one of them being Jane and Our Nobby. They fell again at the last, but still managed to finish in one of the best times of the day, having gained maximum bonus points on the steeplechase. Although Jane's score was not counted on the final day, she became the first woman to win an Olympic team gold medal in eventing. Juliet Jobling Purser had a good round and finished the event in seventh place – the highest individual position achieved by a woman in a three-day event at the Olympics at that time. Her compatriot, Diana Willson, had the misfortune to set out on a cross country when the torrential rain was at its worse, making the going treacherous, but she managed to complete the course. Disaster struck the Irish, however, when Penny Moreton's horse Loughlin fell at the seventh fence and broke his back. He had to be destroyed and Penny Moreton was taken to hospital with several broken ribs.

Mary Gordon Watson, who in 1970 became the first woman to win the World Championships, might have been on the British team in Mexico had she not been injured. Her horse, Cornishman V, went to the Olympics, but Mary had broken her leg in a working hunter class early in the summer and had to forgo her ride on him. Initially, Cornishman was lent to Sgt Ben Jones, who had been teaching Mary, but the partnership did not work out and instead Richard Meade, whose own mount was injured, took the ride on Cornishman and just missed winning an individual bronze medal. It was the start of an outstanding international career for this horse. With Mary back in the saddle he won the subsequent European Championships in Haras du Pin, when Mary was only twenty-one, and the following year made light of the formidable course in Punchestown to take the World Championships. At the 1971 European Championships he helped the British team win the gold medal, finishing fourth individually, and at the Munich Games in 1972, he had an identical result, so that Mary narrowly missed becoming the first woman to win an individual Olympic medal in eventing.

Mary's father had bought Cornishman as a four-year-old, for hunting. But when Mary wanted to take her Pony Club 'A' test and her 14.2hh pony had been borrowed by her younger brother, she began riding Cornishman. He was the first horse she had ridden, and at 17hh was quite a handful for a slightly built, 5ft 5in girl. 'He was very unruly, and I couldn't cope with him to start with. He had an unorthodox style of jumping with his head held high, but he had learnt to look after himself in the hunting field and was surprisingly agile for a big horse.'

The Selection Committee soon realised the potential of this combination and asked Mary to compete *hors concours* at the 1968 Badminton Horse Trials (Cornishman was just out

The Munich Olympic Games, 1972: Mary Gordon-Watson riding her father's Cornishman V. She narrowly missed becoming the first woman to win an individual Olympic medal in eventing.

of novice and had not qualified) with a view to considering them for the Mexico Games. Three fences from the end of the course they fell into the coffin. 'I had been having a fantastic ride, and half way round the course I saw Ben Jones cheering me on. Unfortunately, I thought he was trying to tell me to go faster, so I did, and by the time we reached the coffin we were both exhausted. He hit the first element very hard, and I fell into the ditch on the far side of the fence.'

Cornishman was nine years old at the time, but had started eventing only a year earlier. He had been hobdayed, so his fitness was always a prime consideration. However, he was a brilliant horse across country, and his performance at the World Championships in Punchestown, where he was one of only four horses to go clear over the big, demanding course in appalling weather, was in a class of its own. The results give a good idea of the severity of the course: Richard Meade had a fall but still finished second individually, and Mark Phillips, the third member of the British squad whose results were counted, had two falls, yet even with this cricket score the team won the gold medal. Mary Gordon Watson and Cornishman won the individual title by at least 60 points. When her chance came to compete at the Munich Olympics in 1972, Mary must have been one of the brightest prospects for an individual medal, but as pathfinder for the British team she was caught out – as were countless others – by a tricky drop fence, and had one stop there. By the time Richard Meade rode the course it was clear that the fence should be jumped at the other end and he rode an exemplary round to clinch the individual gold medal as well as the team gold. Mary and Cornishman finished fourth, the best individual place achieved by a woman in an Olympic three-day event.

The following year Cornishman competed successfully in an international event in America, after which he was retired – though he continued to hunt until he was twenty-seven. Mary rode a number of horses following Cornishman's retirement, bringing six up to advanced level, and winning at Wylye with a horse called Highness. She was also responsible for producing Speculator III, the horse on which Richard Meade won at Badminton in 1982. Although Mary has now given up eventing, she has been a member of the Horse Trials Selection Committee for twelve years; she writes books on riding, and teaches both in this country and abroad.

The woman who brought eventing (though the popular press insisted on calling it show jumping) right into the limelight was HRH Princess Anne (now the Princess Royal). In spite of the additional pressures created by performing in the full glare of publicity – a bevy of photographers was always to hand at any event she attended – the Princess managed to compete at the highest levels of the sport with outstanding success. In 1971 she won the individual European title, in 1975 was runner up for the same title, and the following year became the first member of the royal family to represent Britain at an Olympic Games.

Princess Anne's first major success was with a chestnut gelding called Doublet, who was originally bred as a polo pony by HM The Queen. However, when he grew to 16.2hh, too big for polo, the Princess was given the chance to event him. She won on her first outing with him in 1969, and two years later finished fifth at Badminton, the same year in which her future husband, Captain Mark Phillips, won on Great Ovation. The Princess's performance earned her the chance to compete as an individual at the European Champion-

Bronze by Annette Yarrow of HRH Princess Anne on Doublet, the horse on which she won the European Championships in 1971.

ships at Burghley the following September, but two months before the event she had to undergo a major operation which put her appearance at Burghley in jeopardy. Nevertheless, she managed to get herself fit enough for the event, and a superb cross country round on Doublet – the second fastest of the day – followed by a clear in the show jumping secured the individual European title. She and Doublet were shortlisted for the Munich Olympic team the following year but were forced to withdraw when Doublet had leg trouble. He was still not back to his best form by 1973, and so when Princess Anne went to Kiev, Russia, to defend her European title, it was with Goodwill on whom she had finished eighth at Badminton that spring. At the notorious second fence she had crashing fall, badly dislocating her shoulder, and decided to retire as she was not on the team.

The following spring Princess Anne suffered an even greater blow when, exercising Doublet in Windsor Great Park, he broke a hind leg and had to be destroyed. Fortunately, she still had Goodwill who was improving all the time, and her subsequent record with him – twelfth in the 1974 World Championships and second individual in the 1975 European Championships – was consistent enough to secure her a place on the team for Montreal in 1976. The event was a disaster for the British: Lucinda Prior-Palmer (now Mrs Green),

HM The Queen congratulating Princess Anne after her victory in the European Championships at Burghley in 1971.

also making her debut on an Olympic team, had to withdraw when her brilliant horse Be Fair, on whom she had won Badminton three years earlier, slipped a ligament from his hock near the end of the cross country. Princess Anne had a fall with Goodwill and, although concussed, she remounted and finished the course; but when Hugh Thomas's Playamar came down at the water complex and was unable to continue, the British team was eliminated.

It was the last time Princess Anne represented Britain on a championship team, although, following the birth of her two children (Peter in 1977 and Zara in 1981), she has continued to compete in horse trials, mostly at novice and intermediate level. More recently, however, her equestrian talents have taken on a new direction, and on 3 September 1987, she became the first member of the royal family to win a steeplechase under Rules when she rode her own Cnoc na Cuille to first place in the Droitwich Chase at Worcester. Among her numerous activities in the equestrian world the Princess Royal is Patron of the Riding for the Disabled, President of the Windsor Horse Trials and, since December 1986, when she took over from her father, HRH The Duke of Edinburgh, President of the FEI (the International Equestrian Federation).

★   ★   ★

By the 1970s there were a growing number of American women riders competing at international level. In 1979, Torrance Watkins Fleischmann came to England with two horses, Poltroon and Red's Door, and rode them into second and twenty-first places respectively at Burghley. The following year she took Poltroon to the 'Alternative' Olympics in Fontainebleau, when many of the Western nations were boycotting Moscow, and

In the dressage arena at the World championships in Gawler, Australia (1986): Torrance Watkins Fleischmann on Finvarra (USA).

won the individual bronze medal. Had that been a full Olympic event, she would have made history by becoming the first woman to win an individual Olympic medal. Instead, it was left to her compatriot, Karen Stives, to take that honour, when she and Britain's Virginia Holgate won the silver and bronze medals at the Los Angeles Games.

Karen Stives, who was born in New England in 1950, began her equestrian career as a dressage rider, reaching the Grand Prix level, but in 1980 she joined a USET (United States Equestrian Team) training session under their three-day event coach Jack le Goff, and subsequently competed as an individual at the 'Alternative' Olympics, finishing twenty-fourth after a fall at the water complex. The following year her successes at home earned her the title of US Rider of the Year, but in 1982, at the Kentucky three-day event, her career – and her life – were almost ended when her 17hh gelding, Silent Partner, fell at the first cross country fence and landed on her. She was not breathing when the medical team reached her, but she was revived and airlifted to hospital suffering from severe concussion. Three months later she was competing at the World Championships in Luhmühlen, where she finished twenty-fifth.

Karen Stives, individual silver and team gold medallist at the 1984 Los Angeles Olympics.

Consistently good results in the 1984 United States selection trials earned her the chance to ride for her Olympic team, just four years after her international debut. She was the youngest and least experienced of the American squad, but with Ben Arthur, a horse formerly ridden by Mary Hamilton of New Zealand, she produced the best dressage of her team, and then went clear across country to go into the lead. When she entered the show jumping arena in Santa Anita, Los Angeles – the last competitor to go – she had both the individual and team gold medals at stake. It was a frightening responsibility, and despite Karen's calm handling of the occasion, one fence down denied her the individual gold medal. However, her performance was good enough to secure the team gold – by just 3.2 points – from the British, and she had still made history by winning the individual silver medal.

The British team at those Los Angeles Games contained two women who have had by far the greatest impact on the sport of horse trials in recent years – Lucinda Green (née Prior-Palmer) and Virginia Leng (née Holgate). Their achievements have been remarkable. Both riders have been European Champions twice and World Champions once, and both have won Olympic medals. Lucinda Green has won Badminton an unprecedented six times – on six different horses – a record unlikely to be beaten; Virginia (Ginny) Leng has won Burghley on four consecutive years between 1983 and 1986, creating another extraordinary record.

There is a theory that it is better to reach the top initially with just one horse with which the rider has learnt to overcome any problems and setbacks. Those who start out with a number of good horses from which to choose can all too easily switch from one to another as soon as things start going wrong, and they never learn to get to grips with the serious problems. Both Lucinda and Ginny began their careers with one horse that they brought up to top level from novice. In Lucinda's case it was a small chestnut gelding called Be Fair, given to her by her mother in 1968 as a fifteenth birthday present. Be Fair was the only son of Sheila Willcox's event horse Fair and Square, who had won Burghley that year and narrowly missed being selected for the Olympic team. As a precocious two-year-old Fair and Square had jumped into an adjoining field to have an unplanned assignation with a Thoroughbred mare called Happy Reunion, and Be Fair had been the result. He was kept at livery with Mrs Betty Skelton, who had been Lucinda's instructor since she began riding at the age of four, but Be Fair soon proved to be quite a handful. Alan Smith describes those early days: 'When Lucinda took him out for the first time he spooked at every sweet paper, whipped round on the road and, after jumping a small cross country practice fence twice, refused so adamantly to do so again that he reared and went over backwards.

'Friends were brought in to help, and Be Fair was "encouraged" to go forwards, rather than sideways, backwards or even skywards, by being closely pursued by a Land Rover with a lunging whip projected suggestively from a window. In his early days he would even lie down when bored with being lunged in circles. He was enough of a character to test anyone's patience and ingenuity, and in overcoming his quirks, or at least reducing them to a manageable level, Lucinda learned lessons that were to prove invaluable with the many other horses she was able to ride to success.'

Three years later, after many battles and as much help and advice as she could get from top instructors, Lucinda had Be Fair going well enough to be selected for the British team for the Junior European Championships, at which they finished eleventh individually. The following year, 1972, they made their first attempt at Badminton, when Lucinda was just eighteen. They came fifth, despite a run-out at Tom Smith's Walls, and were put on the short-list for the Munich Olympics. Although they failed to be selected for the Olympic team, the next year Lucinda began her foray on Badminton, scoring the first of her six wins. She subsequently went to the European Championships at Kiev, only to have a fall on the cross country, and it was not until 1975 that she gained the first of her European titles. That was in Luhmühlen, when she was on an all-female team with HRH Princess Anne, Janet Hodgson and Sue Hatherley. The team won the silver medal, Lucinda the individual gold, and Princess Anne the individual silver.

From then on the successes continued, and she clocked up an incredible eight consecutive years on the British team. In 1977, when she won Badminton for the third time (with George), and was also placed third on Killaire, women filled the first five places – second was Diana Thorne on the Kingmaker, fourth was Jane Holderness-Roddam (née Bullen) with Warrior, and fifth was Aly Patinson with Carawich. However, it was not all plain sailing for Lucinda: two of her worst moments were the death of Wide Awake when he collapsed

Lucinda Prior-Palmer (now Mrs Green) in 1977, when she was first (with George) and third (with Killaire) at Badminton.

in the arena at Badminton in 1976 during the final lap of honour, and the moment when Be Fair broke down at the end of the cross country at the Montreal Olympics.

By 1978 the costs of keeping and competing on good horses were becoming an increasing burden, and Lucinda took the decision to look for financial support. It was a plunge in at the deep end, for no event rider had taken on commercial backing before, and she was the first to experience the pressures of riding for a sponsor. But Lucinda has never been afraid to tread new paths in the eventing world or to give voice on issues close to her heart. In 1980 when the Russians invaded Afghanistan, Lucinda spoke out strongly in favour of boycotting the Moscow Games, and two years later, when the Midland Bank decided to drop its umbrella sponsorship of eventing she was one of the prime movers in encouraging the sport to open its doors to a whole range of commercial sponsors. In 1984 she represented Britain for a second time at an Olympic Games (it would have been her third consecutive time had the 1980 Olympics not been boycotted, for she rode at the 'Alternative' Olympics at Fontainebleau). She came sixth in Los Angeles with her world champion horse Regal Realm, and helped Britain to win the silver medal. On the team with her was Ginny Leng, who had won the individual bronze medal and who has been stealing the eventing limelight ever since.

Like Lucinda, Ginny began her eventing career on a complete novice. Dubonnet, known as Dubby, had arrived at the Holgate's home at the age of six months – a bargain that

The all-female British team at Frauenfeld (1983), when Britain won the silver medal. From left to right: Virginia Holgate (now Mrs Leng), Lorna Clarke, Lucinda Green and Diana Clapham.

Ginny's grandfather had picked up at the local cattle market for a mere £35. Dubby's dam was a Dartmoor pony, but his sire, Golden Surprise, was also the sire of Mary Gordon Watson's great horse Cornishman V, so the Holgate family followed Mary's eventing career with interest.

Ginny's father served with the Royal Marines, and the family did not settle in England until Ginny was sixteen, by which time Dubby was five years old and had already been broken in. Eager to get started on him, Ginny entered him in his first show jumping class at a local gymkhana, where they were duly eliminated. Her first attempt at eventing was equally unsuccessful when they were eliminated on the cross country at a Pony Club event at Killerton in the autumn of 1971. However, the Strachan sisters, Sally and Clarissa (the latter competed on the World Championship team in 1986) had by this time taken Ginny under their wing, and gradually began to mould her and Dubby into a useful combination. Within a year Ginny had successfully completed the Tidworth three-day event, and was chosen to ride as an individual at the Junior European Championships. She fell at the third to last fence on the cross country, but, by the following year (1973), she and Dubby had really got their act together and took both the team and individual gold medal at the Junior Championships in Pompadour, France.

Their first outing at Badminton, in the spring of 1974, was not so good. As they jumped the Huntsman's Leap the reins slipped through Ginny's hands and she lost control of Dubby, who went dashing into some nearby bushes. It was some time before she was able to bring him back in hand, re-emerge from the undergrowth and find her way back onto the cross country, but she did finish the course. The next year the weather was so wet that Badminton had to be cancelled after the dressage, and Ginny lost her chance of improving her performance there. But things had been going well, and by the beginning of 1976 she had been long listed for the Montreal Olympics with a horse called Jason. It was while competing with him at a one day event at Ermington, Devon, that disaster struck: 'Jason left one leg on the wrong side of the second fence and turned over. As I went flying through the air, I put my left arm out to break my fall and failed to bend my elbow. So the impact of the fall smashed my wrist. The whole arm had been rotated so that when I sat on the grass, wondering what injury I might have done myself, the elbow was pointing up instead of down.'

Her arm had been broken in twenty-three places and the nerves so badly damaged that amputation was seriously considered. But Ginny's mother, Heather, persuaded the surgeon at Plymouth Naval Hospital to try saving the arm, even if it had to be paralysed, and in a four-hour operation he managed to piece the broken bones together. It was weeks before Ginny was able to regain enough feeling in her fingers to be able even to pick

(*right*) Two of the three female members of the British team at the 1984 Olympics: Diana Clapham on Windjammer (*above*), and Lucinda Green on Regal Realm.

up a glass, but gradually she nursed the injured arm back to use, and in five months was back in competition. Not long after, however, she came close to giving up eventing. Dubby and Jason had both been retired, and her next hope, Tio Pepe, broke down on the steeplechase course at Badminton in 1977. 'I was left in gloom and despair. In little more

(*above*) The third female member of the British team at the 1984 Olympics: Virginia Leng on Priceless, and (*right*) Rachel Hunt on Aloaf at Stowell Park, 1987.

than a year I'd smashed my arm and seen my three advanced horses pushed into early retirement.' It was Lucinda Green who encouraged her to keep going, inviting her to join a riders' seminar that she was giving at Wylye. 'That seminar was the turning point for me. I shall always be immensely grateful to Lucinda for helping me to turn a difficult corner and putting me back on the right road.'

By then Ginny had begun working on two youngsters that her mother had bought – Priceless and Night Cap – the two horses that were to bring her so much success. They were the same age, and both were sons of Diana Scott's stallion Ben Faerie, but there the similarities ended. 'If Priceless were human, he would have made a good sergeant-major. He'd be butch, short, muscular and aggressive. Night Cap is much more the officer type; incredibly polite, very good-looking and far more sensitive than his bossy stable companion.' With these two horses Ginny represented Britain at every international championship from 1981 to 1987, and never came home without a medal.

Her outstanding success is due in no small way to her determination and her ability to profit from her own mistakes, as well as learning from others. She has also had the benefit of a tightly knit team to look after and train her horses. Her mother, Heather, is responsible for feeding and fitness, and in this area no stone is left unturned to ensure that the horses reach their peak for an event, while Dorothy (Dot) Willis is Ginny's trainer and mentor. Ginny has said that she finds it remarkable that three such strong-willed women can work together in harmony, but they succeed because they respect each other's knowledge and do not infringe on one another's patch. It is an invincible team; these three women have created one of the strongest forces ever to have taken on the eventing world.

Margit Otto Crespin (France) competing with Corlandus at Goodwood in 1987 when she won the individual European Dressage title.

Gee Armytage riding Gee A in the Mildmay Chase in 1987, when she became the first woman to win against the professionals at Cheltenham.

The Princess Royal winning the Dresden Diamond Stakes at Ascot, 1987, with Ten No Trumps.

CHAPTER FIVE
DRESSAGE

Women have won more Olympic medals in dressage than in any other equestrian sport. Between 1952 and 1984 they gained three gold, three silver and one bronze individual medals, and numerous team medals. At the 1972 Munich Games, twenty-one of the thirty-three riders were women, and both the current World and European Champions are women. It is hardly surprising that dressage has become known as the sport of the 'Amazones'.

It was not always the case. The earliest Olympic competitions were open only to cavalry officers, and women were not allowed to take part until 1952. When they did, they made an immediate impact, for at those Helsinki Games the Danish rider Lis Hartel won the individual silver medal, thus becoming the first woman to be awarded an Olympic medal in an equestrian sport. Her achievement was all the more remarkable because eight years earlier she had suffered a severe attack of polio that had left her almost completely paralysed. She was twenty-three at the time, and expecting a baby.

Before her child was born Lis Hartel had learned to lift her arm and use her thigh muscles, and after giving birth to a healthy daughter she regained enough control over her limbs to start crawling, and then to walk on crutches. She was so determined to ride again that she insisted on getting back on a horse before she could walk properly. The effort was so exhausting that she had to rest for two weeks before she could try again. Her perseverance eventually paid off: three years after the polio attack she rode in the Scandinavian championships, finishing second in the women's dressage. Although she remained paralysed below the knees, and had to be helped on and off her horse, she was selected to represent Denmark in 1952 Olympics. The presentation of her silver medal in Helsinki, where she rode a horse called Jubilee, was one of the most emotional moments in Olympic history. She had overcome a terrible handicap, worked her way up to international standard, and had achieved the first Olympic success for the 'Amazones'. That success was repeated four years later in Stockholm, where once again she won the silver medal on Jubilee, and, again, was beaten by the Swedish rider Henri Saint Cyr.

The German team at Stockholm was made up entirely of women, and one of them, Liselott Linsenhoff, won the individual bronze medal. This young German rider was later to become the first woman to win an individual Olympic gold medal in equestrian sport, but she had to wait another sixteen years before creating that particular piece of history.

Dressage in Britain at that time was just beginning to get off the ground. Two women, Mrs Lorna Johnstone and Mrs V. D. S. Williams, mother of the late Dorian Williams, had represented Britain at the Stockholm Games, finishing twenty-first and twenty-fifth respectively out of a field of thirty-six. 'The test was diabolical,' according to Mrs Johnstone.

Lis Hartel, the first woman to win an Olympic medal in an equestrian sport. She overcame a serious polio attack to gain the individual silver medal at the 1952 Games.

'We had to do one-time changes on a circle. It was very, very difficult.' A comment on the British performance was made by Mrs H. W. Inderwick in the 1957 *Horseman's Yearbook*: 'To match our two British horses against such opposition, when between them they can only number six international contests – not counting our own where the standard has never been very high – was asking a great deal. Add to this the fact that it was the first opportunity either had had of competing in a Grand Prix and also that, unlike so many of their rivals, they had trained their horses themselves, does make one realise what excellent performances they gave to stand so high in the list.'

Britain's lack of success at international level was largely the result of disinterest and inexperience. The riders did not benefit from the Continental traditions of *haute école*, and most of them were keener on hunting and jumping anyway. 'Not many men were interested in dressage,' says Mrs Johnstone, who, from the early 1950s to the mid 1970s was Britain's most successful dressage rider. She won the National Championships a staggering thirteen times (the next best record is that of Jennie Loriston-Clarke, who, up to 1988, had won it six times), and in 1972 made history by being the oldest Olympic competitor at the Munich Games. She was seventy when she rode El Farruco to twelfth place, which was the best performance by a British rider.

Lorna Johnstone was born on 4 September 1902, in Yorkshire. She learnt to ride and hunt as a small child, and grew up with a great love of horses. Every horse she has owned has been painted, and the pictures adorn the walls of her house at Hanley Castle, near Worcester. They include two horses that she rode in India, when her husband was posted there with the army, numerous hunters and the more famous names from her dressage days – Greatheart, Conquistador, Rosie Dream, El Guapo, El

98

Farruco. Her dressage career began with Greatheart with whom she competed in driving events as well as dressage and 'combined training' competitions. It was with this horse that she won the first one-day event to be held in this country, at Wellesbourne in 1946. In spite of this success (and, incidently, victory in a novice point-to-point while in India), Mrs Johnstone was not keen on jumping, and decided to concentrate on dressage. Ten years later she was selected to represent Britain at the Stockholm Olympics, and in 1968 went to Mexico with El Guapo, where she finished thirteenth.

At the subsequent Olympic Games, in Munich, she was on the team with Domini Lawrence and Jennie Loriston-Clarke, the latter making her debut on an Olympic team. For Jennie, it was not a particularly auspicious start to what has since become an outstanding dressage career: she finished twenty-fourth on Mrs Steele's Kadett and nearly caused the British squad to get caught in the cross-fire between the German police and terrorists. The Arab terrorists struck the Olympic Village, killing eleven Israelis, on the first day of the dressage competition. 'It was a traumatic day,' recounts Jennie. 'We had been up at 5 a.m. to prepare the horses for their tests, and when that was over we were not allowed back into the Olympic Village because of the terrorists. When we eventually got in, at about 8 p.m., I passed out while we were having supper and had to be carried across the area occupied by terrorists to my room.' Jennie's blackout was, unbeknown to her at the time, caused by damage to her neck, which she had injured while riding a bucking horse. She had been suffering from severe headaches for the past year, but her doctor had been unable to pinpoint the problem. As soon as she returned from Munich she was taken to a London hospital, only to be told to come back the following week for a scan, as she 'might have a tumour on the brain'. It was a great relief when the trouble was eventually attributed to her neck.

Lorna Johnstone with El Guapo, the horse she rode at the 1968 Mexico Olympics. In 1972, when she was seventy years old, she came twelfth at the Munich Games.

Surrounded by ponies from an early age, Jennie's background was almost bound to lead her into a career with horses. One of six children, she was brought up at Catherston Manor, Dorset, where her parents, Colonel and Mrs John Bullen, founded the famous Catherston stud that Jennie now runs from her home in the New Forest. Her mother was an artist as well as a talented horsewoman, and all the children rode – three of them at Olympic level. Michael Bullen was a member of the British three-day-event team in Rome in 1960, and Jane (now Mrs Holderness-Roddam) was on the event team that won the gold medal at the 1968 Olympics. Jennie has competed on the dressage team at three Olympic Games – 1972, 1976 and 1984 – and the 'alternative' Olympics at Goodwood in 1980, where she finished in sixth place.

As a youngster, Jennie was an all round horsewoman. She evented, show jumped and, at the age of seventeen, went point-to-pointing to gain her Duke of Edinburgh Award. Riding a mare called Three Royals, who she had trained herself, Jennie spent two seasons riding point-to-points, and was unplaced only once. As for dressage, 'In the back of my mind I had always thought that it was a sissy sport, although I enjoyed training horses. But in 1952 I saw Madame Hartel give a display at the Horse of the Year Show, which was beautiful.' Jennie's mother had already taught her to do some of the more advanced movements on her successful show hack, Desert Storm, who won at the Horse of the Year Show on three consecutive years, so when Jennie started competing at medium level dressage she found herself among the prize winners straight away. Following Desert Storm was a thoroughbred stallion called Xenocles, who did almost as well in horse trials (coming fourth at the Tidworth three-day event) as he did in dressage, though he never competed at international level.

The German-bred Kadett was Jennie's ride for the 1972 Olympics, but her best horse to date is undoubtedly the brilliant stallion Dutch Courage with whom she won the bronze medal at the World Championships in 1978 – a performance that put British dressage on the map. She bought him on her way back from a European show, having decided to make a detour via Holland. 'I wanted either a stallion or mare, so that the horse could be used at stud as well as in competition, and I had not been able to find a good animal in England at a sensible price. We only saw Dutch Courage trot down a road in-hand, in a snow storm, but he moved so well that I knew he was an exceptional horse.'

In 1984 Dutch Courage was one of Britain's great hopes for the Los Angeles Olympics, and, together with Christopher Bartle's Wily Trout and Jane Bartle-Wilson's Pinocchio, it looked as if Britain was really in with a chance of winning a team medal. But, two weeks before he was due to fly out to Los Angeles, Dutch Courage contracted a virus that affected his joints, and he was unable to go. This serious blow was offset to some extent by Diana Mason's generous offer to lend her talented young horse, Prince Consort, to Jennie to ride. With only ten days in which to get to know Prince Consort – an inexperienced horse who had performed his first Grand Prix only five months earlier – Jennie did remarkably well to produce a reasonable test on a horse that was clearly daunted by the occasion, but the British team was no longer in contention for a medal. The following summer Dutch Courage made his final appearance at Goodwood to mark his retirement from competitive work.

Apart from his outstanding dressage career, which included the 'Alternative' Olympics, and six consecutive wins in the British National Championships, as well as the individual bronze at the 1978 World Championships, Dutch Courage has been a highly successful stallion at stud. Two of his progeny, Dutch Gold and Catherston Dutch Bid, are now at Grand Prix level, and a third, Dancing Storm, a grandson of Desert Storm, is regarded by Jennie as a future star in dressage. Dutch Courage is also used as a schoolmaster for Jennie's daughter, Lizzie, and by students attending courses at Catherston. Out of some forty-five horses belonging to Jennie and her husband, ten are kept for teaching students.

Jennie Loriston-Clarke riding Dutch Courage with whom she won the bronze medal at the 1978 World Championships.

Jane Bartle-Wilson and Pinocchio at the 1984 Los Angeles Olympics.

'I am keen to promote the sport and to help young riders,' says Jennie. 'We've got good horses in this country, but it's not so easy finding the right riders.'

It was as a result of Jennie's initiative and organisational talents that a performance horse sale was held in this country for the first time in 1987. The idea was to encourage breeders to produce competition horses and to provide them with a good marketing outlet. Potential sale horses were carefully examined by Jennie who then went to Stoneleigh with a team of riders and grooms to spend two weeks training them. In this way she got to know all the horses, and was able to advise prospective buyers on what might suit them as well as allowing them to try out the horses. Not surprisingly, the sale was a great success, and there are plans to hold it on an annual basis.

When Jennie competed in her first Olympics in 1972, the German rider Liselott Linsenhoff made history by becoming the first woman rider to win an individual Olympic gold medal. On a horse called Piaffe, she helped the West German team to take the silver medal, and beat the good Russian woman, Elena Petouchkova, on Pepel to first place as an indi-

The first woman to win an individual Olympic gold medal for an equestrian sport: Liselott Linsenhoff (West Germany). She rode a horse called Piaffe to win at Munich in 1972.

vidual. It was Liselott's final Olympic appearance in an outstanding international career that spanned five Olympic Games, and which included individual gold and bronze Olympic medals, a team gold and two team silver Olympic medals, and two European individual gold medals. Her victory at Munich began a succession of female dominance at Olympic level, which was not broken until 1984 when Reiner Klimke triumphed in Los Angeles.

At the 1976 Olympics the Swiss rider, Christine Stückelberger made her mark on the dressage world by winning the individual gold medal from two of Germany's top riders, Harry Boldt and Reiner Klimke. Christine, who is only 5ft 4in tall, fair-haired and light-boned, always looked frail and vulnerable on the powerful 16hh Granat, yet she was able to produce outstanding performances from him. He had a reputation for being a bit wild, and it was not unknown for him to take advantage of his strength and run off with his diminutive rider. When Christine first saw him she realised that he was better suited to a strong man, but she was so impressed by his powerful action that she decided to buy

(*left*) Christine Stückelberger (Switzerland), winner of the individual Olympic gold medal in 1976, and (*below*) Mrs Jook Hall with Conversana Caprice, the horse with whom she represented Britain at three consecutive Olympic Games.

him. Her perseverance in training this difficult and temperamental horse paid off, for, as well as winning the gold medal in Montreal, her successes with him included individual victories at the 1975 and 1977 European Championships, the 1978 World Championships, and the 'Alternative' Olympics at Goodwood in 1980.

From 1956 Britain has sent dressage riders to every Olympic Games (including the 'Alternative' Olympics), and until 1984 those riders had always been women. One of the most consistent performers was Mrs Jook Hall, who represented Britain at three consecutive Olympics – Rome, Tokyo and Mexico – on each occasion riding Conversana Caprice. She would have been included in the 1972 Munich team also, but her top horse at that time, Detective, died of colic just three weeks before the Olympics. When her bad luck

The 1986 World Champion, Anne Grethe Jensen (The Netherlands) riding Marzog.

continued with the death of another horse as a result of cancer, Mrs Hall decided to give up competitive riding. She has since become an international judge, both for pure dressage and for the dressage test of three-day events.

The highest placing ever achieved by a British dressage rider at an Olympic games is sixth. This was accomplished in 1984 – by a man. Christopher Bartle was the person who broke the female domination of dressage in Britain, and with his brilliant horse Wily Trout (now retired), became the top British rider. When he won the National Championships in 1984, he was the first man to do so for thirty-five years.

Female domination of the sport is probably more pronounced in Britain than any other country, but even on the Continent women are winning more often than the men. The current World Champion is the Danish rider Anne Grethe Jensen, and women filled all three individual medal positions at the 1987 European Championships at Goodwood. (Unfortunately, six months after the contest, the winner of the bronze medal, Christine Stückelberger, was disqualified because traces of theobromine had been found in her horse's blood.) It is a sport that seems to attract women, despite being more physically demanding than it looks. It is often the case that women can succeed on a horse that would not be strong enough to cope with the demands of complex dressage movements if ridden by a heavy man. On the other hand, a man's weight can be used to good advantage: Mrs P. J. Gold, one of Britain's most experienced dressage judges, considers that men nearly always produce better pirouettes – a movement that requires the horse to really lower its hindquarters.

Women riders are well aware that they do not possess the physical capabilities to force a horse to do something it would rather not do, so they must rely on guile and intuition, and must, above all, be patient. When it comes to the crunch, men may be tempted to force an issue by using strength, which could give them more problems in the long run. It is, after all, the partnership that counts, an understanding between horse and rider. If that is well established, there is no reason why women, though physically weaker, should not succeed in any equestrian sport.

CHAPTER SIX
RACING

'Are your ready for your steeplechase, Lorraine, Lorraine, Lorrée?
Barum, Barum, Barum, Barum, Barum, Barum, Barree
You're booked to ride your capping race today at Coulter Lee,
You're booked to ride Vindictive for all the world to see,
To keep him straight, to keep him first, and win the race for me.'

She clasped her new-born baby, poor Lorraine, Lorraine, Lorrée.
'I cannot ride Vindictive, as any man might see,
And I will not ride Vindictive, with this baby on my knee;
He's killed a boy, he's killed a man and why must he kill me?'

'Unless you ride Vindictive, Lorraine, Lorraine, Lorrée,
Unless you ride Vindictive today at Coulter Lee,
And land him safe across the brook, and win the blank for me,
It's you may keep your baby, for you'll get no help from me.'

'That husbands could be cruel,' said Lorraine, Lorraine, Lorrée,
'That husbands could be cruel, I have known for seasons three;
But oh! to ride Vindictive while a baby cries for me,
And be killed across a fence for all the world to see!'

She mastered young Vindictive – Oh! the gallant lass was she,
And kept him straight and won the race as near as near could be;
But he killed her at the brook, against a pollard willow tree.
Oh! he killed her at the brook, the brute, for all the world to see,
And no one but the baby cried for poor Lorraine, Lorrée.

Charles Kingsley (1819–1875): *Lorraine, Lorraine, Lorrée*

Charles Kingsley must have had a vivid imagination, for it is unlikely that he ever saw a woman riding in a steeplechase in the nineteenth century. There seem to be no records of females in early steeplechase races, although how many unofficial 'races' across country were held is anyone's guess, and it is quite possible that one or two women rode in these. In 1725 a Ladies' Plate was run on Ripon Heath in Yorkshire in which, it is said, some of the women were bold enough to ride astride, but since no other ladies' races are recorded one can only assume that it was not a huge success.

The only woman whose name appeared in the Racing Calendar in the nineteenth century was Mrs Alicia Thornton, who ran a four-mile match against her brother-in-law, Captain Flint, on York's Knavesmire course in 1804. The prospect of a woman appearing on a racecourse at that time caused tremendous interest, 'so much so', wrote John Orton in his *Turf Annals of York and Doncaster*, 'that an assemblage amounting nearly to one hundred thousand persons attended the course to witness the contest, and the aid of the military (the 16th Light Dragoons) was required to assist in keeping the course.'

There seems to have been some question over Mrs Thornton's real identity. Orton wrote that she was, in fact, the 'Chère Amie' of Colonel Thornton, a prominent sportsman of his day, and her real name was Alicia Meynell, the daughter of a respectable watch-maker

A contemporary cartoon of the match between Alicia Thornton and Captain Flint in 1804.

from Norwich. She was 'about twenty-two years of age, very handsome, fair complexion, light hair, blue eyes, and very fascinating.' Another contemporary, but anonymous, statement disputes Orton's theory, saying that 'there is no doubt that the marriage ceremony was duly performed', and that Mrs Thorton's 'riding qualifications were known far and wide, and when it was stated that she was going to ride at a public race the news spread throughout the country like wildfire.'

> *See the course throng'd with gazers, and lots of 'Old Rakes',*
> *To view the 'beautiful Heroine' start for the stakes;*
> *With Handkerchiefs waving, the spectators all clap,*
> *Half dressed like a jockey, with her whip and her cap.*
> *With spirits like fire, behold her mount the gay prad,*
> *And the cheers and the smiles make her heart light and glad;*
> *And Mrs Thornton's 'the favourite' through thick and through thin,*
> *And the swell and the jockeys all bet that she'll win.*

Mrs Thornton led for the first three miles, but had to concede victory to Captain Flint in the last mile when her horse went lame. However, a report in a York newspaper concluded: 'Never, surely, did a woman ride in better style. It is difficult to say whether her horsemanship or her dress and beauty were most admired. She gained the admiration of all, and much disappointment was felt by the immense crowd of spectators at her not winning her match.'

A second challenge was laid down by Mrs Thornton, but it never materialised because Colonel Thorton had apparently not paid Captain Flint the £1,000 wager for the first race. At the York summer meeting 'A terrible row took place at the stand, . . . Mr Flint came to the racecourse with a whip, which he applied to the colonel's back with great activity, in the presence of a crowd of ladies. . . . He was arrested by order of the Lord Mayor and several magistrates who were present.' However, in 1805, Mrs Thornton rode in, and won, a two-mile match at York against one of the leading jockeys of the time, Francis Buckle. A contemporary report describes the race: 'This was the first occasion a lady had ever displayed her riding powers against such a master of the art as the renowned Mr F. Buckle. Mrs Thornton, dressed in a purple cap and waistcoat, nankeen coloured skirts, purple shoes and embroidered stockings. . . . Immediately Mrs Thornton took the lead, which she kept for some time. Buckle then put in trial his jockeyship, and passed the petticoat and kept the lead for a few lengths, when Mrs Thorton's, we may truly say, horsemanship, pushed forwards, and came in in a style far superior to any-

A commemorative goblet of Mrs Thornton's challenge.

thing of the kind we ever witnessed, winning her race by half a neck. The manner of Mrs Thornton's riding is certainly of the first description; indeed her close seat and perfect management of her horse, her bold and steady jockeyship on one of the most crowded courses we have for a long time seen, elicited the highest admiration, and on her winning she was hailed with the most deafening shouts and congratulations.'

This was the last time the 'fair Alicia' appeared on a racecourse and, indeed, the last time any woman rode under the auspices of the Jockey Club for at least 165 years. At the beginning of this century, when point-to-point became formally established, women did at least have an outlet for their race riding talents, but even here they were restricted to 'Ladies' Races' for nearly forty years. As for the Flat and National Hunt fixtures, these remained the preserve of men until as late as the 1970s, when the last male bastions of the Jockey Club finally crumbled to allow women on the racecourse.

★   ★   ★

Before that historic day in 1972, when women rode in their first Flat race under Jockey Club jurisdiction, they had already made their mark on the racing world as owners and

The Great Seal of Queen Anne, who was the instigator of racing at Ascot.

trainers, though their influence had been relatively slight until the twentieth century. The exceptions were the female monarchs who had a significant hand in directing the fortunes of racing. Elizabeth I had inherited her father's passion for racing, and kept stables at Eltham, Kent, and at Greenwich Palace. She also maintained breeding studs at Hampton Court, Tutbury, in Staffordshire, and at Cole Park, Malmesbury, though it is clear from the lists of mares and youngstock that not all the animals at these studs were bred for racing. The studs at Malmesbury and Tutbury were later dispersed, the latter by order of the Commonwealth in 1650. But after the Restoration some of the Tutbury mares were recovered and sent to Hampton Court, and by the time Queen Anne came to the throne in 1702 the stables were fully reinstated and Newmarket was already established as the headquarters of racing.

Queen Anne adored hunting and racing. When she was older, and unable to ride a horse, she would terrify her attendants by hunting in a small, specially designed carriage, which she drove at hair-raising speeds. According to Elizabeth Strickland: 'She followed the chase in a light, one-horse chair constructed to hold only herself and built with enormously high wheels. In this extraordinary and dangerous hunting equipage she was known to drive her fine strong hackney forty or fifty miles in an afternoon.'

On 11 August 1711, Queen Anne inaugurated the first race meeting at Ascot. The main race was 'Her Majesty's plate of a hundred guineas to be run for round the new Heath on Ascot Common . . .'. Meetings were attended by fashionable ladies, often mounted. On the day before the first meeting at Ascot the Queen went to inspect the course, and an account of the visit describes the outfit worn by the Queen's maid of honour, Miss Forester. 'The latter rode a palfrey and was dressed like a man in a long white riding coat, full-flapped waistcoat, court hat bound with gold lace (point to the front) and a flowing periwig.'

Queen Anne also took an interest in racing at York, where she presented to the race committee a gold challenge cup, valued at 100 guineas, to be competed for annually by horses up to the age of six. The race fell into some disrepute in 1714 when the jockeys of the two leading horses, Duchess and Foxhunter, were both guilty of foul riding in the final heat, and actually fought each other while still mounted. The owners, Mr Childers and Mr Peirson, both claimed the cup, which had to be put into the custody of the Lord Mayor of the City of York while a lawsuit was held. The Queen never knew of the scandal, for she died while the York race meeting was still in progress, though not before she had heard the news that her bay colt, Star, had won the £14 plate.

When, over a century later, Queen Victoria succeeded to the throne the Hampton Court Stud was immediately dispersed, despite a petition to the government signed by influential members of the Jockey Club, pointing out the value of Thoroughbred breeding. It was apparent that the Queen had scant interest in racing, and during her reign it became even less acceptable for women to enjoy an active involvement in the sport. At first it had looked as if the Queen might patronise the turf, for in 1840 she announced her intention to visit the Derby at Epsom. According to Michael Wynn Jones, 'to ensure the success of her visit Epsom dressed itself up with awnings and crimson carpets, flags and cascades of flowers; yet almost inevitably things went wrong.'[11] The crowd had got wind of the royal approach route and frustrated all the police efforts to clear a path; the saddling enclosure had to be moved at the last minute and the catering arrangements for lunch had not satisfied the Queen. It was the last time she ever set foot at Epsom.

In 1926 Lady Augusta Fane wrote in her memoirs: 'Racing was not considered a sport suitable for young ladies . . . Of course an exception was made for Ascot, which was then a very select Meeting, and ultra smart. In 1875 there were not more than a hundred ladies in the Royal Enclosure, and my mother told me that when she went with my father in 1858 there were only fifteen or twenty. . . .'

Since the involvement of women in the racing world met with disapproval, two of the most outstanding female racehorse owners of the nineteenth century ran their horses under male pseudonyms. The Duchess of Montrose, or 'Mr Manton', was one of the most successful racehorse breeders of her time, and when her stud was dispersed at her death in 1894 the influence of her bloodstock lines continued for many generations. Two of her most notable horses were Sefton, winner of the 1878 Derby, and St Marguerite, winner of the One Thousand Guineas. The Duchess, who married three times, was clearly one of the more colourful characters of the racing world, and, despite the pseudonym, it was well known that 'Mr Manton's' horses were really those of the Duchess. She knew far more about racing and breeding than most owners, and frequently clashed with her trainers and jockeys over the preparation and running of her horses. Consequently, she went through a number of trainers in her lifetime, among them Alec Taylor, said to be the only man who could come off best in an argument with her.

Her distinctive racing colours of scarlet jacket and cap earned her the nickname of 'Carrie Red'. Fred Archer often rode for her, and, after the Duke had died (and before Fred Archer's own tragic marriage), it was rumoured that she was going to marry him. It was said, however, that he would have nothing to do with the idea on discovering that the match would not make him a Duke. Instead, in 1876, the Duchess married W. Stirling Crawfurd, a member of the Jockey Club and, by all accounts, quite a dandy. He had dyed gold hair and at race meetings always wore a stock and a homburg hat. Following his death, the duchess, then aged seventy, married 24-year-old Henry Milner.

Another outstanding owner in this era was 'Mr Jersey', better known as the Jersey belle, Lillie Langtry. Contrary to the Duchess of Montrose, her racecourse successes appeared to be more a matter of luck than the result of knowledge and good judgement. Indeed, she may never have become a racehorse owner had she not been offered a gift of a two-year-old colt called Milford, who promptly won his first race for her at Kempton Park. Lillie Langtry never went to see her new acquisition racing, but by the end of his first season Milford had won £8,000 in stake money, so it is hardly surprising that Mrs Langtry warmed to the idea of racehorse ownership. She soon had some twenty horses in training and a string of successes to her name that included the Goodwood Plate and Cup, the Ascot Gold Cup and two wins in the Cesarewitch.

By the turn of the century eighty-one women had their names registered with Weatherbys, and in 1917, when the Thoroughbred Breeders' Association was formed in response to the War Cabinet's decision to stop racing, the Dowager Marchioness of Londonderry became one of its first committee members. By now women breeders had begun to make their mark on racing, showing that their judgement and expertise in this field could match, and often better, their male counterparts. Lady Meux, whose racing name was 'Mr Theobalds', had already become the first woman to breed a Derby winner when the three-year-old Volodyovski ran to victory in 1901; and in 1918, five years after the suffragette Emily Wilding Davison had died after running in front of the horses at Tattenham Corner, Lady James Douglas's Gainsborough won the Derby, the Two Thousand Guineas, and the St Leger. In 1915 Lady Nelson was the first woman to own the winner of the Grand National when her six-year-old Ally Sloper finished ahead of Jacobus despite nearly unseating his jockey, Jack Anthony, at the second fence. Four years later Mrs Hugh Peel had the distinction of owning the Grand National winner on two consecutive occasions when her Poethlyn, ridden by Ernie Piggott, grandfather of Lester, won in 1918 and 1919. The Hon. Dorothy Paget was another to own a Grand National winner when her five times Cheltenham Gold Cup victor Golden Miller triumphed at Aintree in 1934.

Lady James Douglas with Gainsborough, winner of the Derby, the Two Thousand Guineas and the St Leger in 1918.

Miss Paget, a wealthy daughter of Lord Queenborough, raced horses for thirty years, during which time she gained a reputation for heavy gambling, both on her own horses and others, and driving cars very fast. She was a formidable character, and few people were able to stand up to her demands and eccentricities. One person who did was Ruth Charlton, Miss Paget's secretary for eighteen years, but she had joined Miss Paget's staff only after being bullied into the job by her employer. It was the same story on many other occasions, with Miss Paget always getting her way. She invariably left too little time to get from one place to another, so that Ruth Charlton had to ensure that her journeys could be made with the minimum of delay. As Caroline Ramsden, in her book *Ladies in Racing*, explains: 'These near-royal progresses made a great deal of difference to her enjoyment of a day's racing. The best of them occurred at Stratford-on-Avon, to which she had travelled by air, Ruth meeting her with a car at the aerodrome. She was anxious to get away as quickly as possible after racing, and left arrangements to Ruth, who asked the officer in charge of the police if he could do anything about it; he arranged an escort which flashed them through the town as if they had been in open country. Miss Paget was delighted, "Excellent Ruth – in future you must always do this."'

The enthusiasm for racing shown by King George VI was shared by his wife and eldest daughter, and in 1949 Princess Elizabeth became the joint owner with her mother of a steeplechaser, Monaveen, which she ran under her own name. Monaveen's first outing for his new owners was in the Chichester Handicap Chase at Fontwell, where he won easily from a field of three. A second place at Liverpool was followed by three consecutive wins – one at Sandown and two at Hurst Park – and then a successful outing in the Grand National where he finished fifth. The following spring Lord Mildmay, the man who had initially encouraged Princess Elizabeth's involvement in racing, drowned while swimming. One outcome of this tragedy was the the French-bred horse, Manicou, which Lord Mildmay had left behind with his trainer Peter Cazalet, was subsequently bought by the Queen (now the Queen Mother). She promptly registered the colours of 'blue, buff stripes, blue sleeves, black cap with a gold tassel', which had first been used by her great uncle, Lord Strathmore. In November of that year Manicou won a three mile chase at Kempton, giving its owner the distinction of being the first Queen of England to have her colours successfully carried since Queen Anne's Star won at York in 1714.

One of the most famous of the Queen Mother's horses was Devon Loch, the chaser that had looked certain to win the 1956 Grand National until, fifty yards from the finishing post, he inexplicably staggered and fell. Seemingly none the worse for this unfortunate experience, Devon Loch was kept in training and won a hurdle race in Nottingham the following October. He ran in three more steeplechases, winning one and coming second in the other two, but in the Mildmay Memorial Chase at Sandown, on 19 January 1957, he broke down at the penultimate fence. He had been in the lead, and managed to scramble over the last, to limp home in fourth place. To the onlookers at Sandown it must have augured the end for this brave horse, but the Queen Mother was reluctant to have him destroyed, having already suffered the loss of her brilliant 'chaser, Monaveen, when he broke a leg in the Queen Elizabeth Chase in 1951. She sent Devon Loch to the trainer, Norah Wilmot, to attempt a cure; remarkably, after a year in her care, he was pronounced fit and ready to race again. He did not, however, go back to the racecourse, and instead went into honourable retirement as a hack for trainer Noel Murless.

Among the Queen Mother's other successful horses have been Gay Record, who registered the hundredth racing triumph for his owner when he won the Sevenoaks Handicap Chase at Folkestone in 1964, and Game Spirit, whose prolific wins included the 1974 Cheltenham Gold Cup. Sadly, this good 'chaser died of a lung haemorrhage just after completing the $2\frac{1}{2}$ mile race at Newbury in 1977. More recently the Queen Mother has

(*right*) HM The Queen at the 200th Derby, Epsom, 1979.

taken an interest in breeding jumpers, and one of her top brood mares, Queen of the Isle, is the dam of Inch Arran, Colonious, Isle of Man and Queen's College, between them winners of over forty races over jumps.

When George VI died in February 1952 his daughter inherited the Sandringham Stud with twenty mares and nine home-bred horses in training. The entrance to the stud is dominated by a larger than life-size bronze of the 1896 Derby winner Persimmon, owned and bred by King Edward VII, a reminder that HM The Queen has yet to achieve her greatest racing ambition: to breed and race the winner of the Derby. She has won all the Classics except this one. Auerole, one of the horses inherited from her father, came close to realising this ambition within a week of the Queen's coronation in June 1953, but he was beaten by four lengths by Pinza, ridden by Sir Gordon Richards. Nevertheless that year the Queen won her first race at Royal Ascot – the Hunt Cup with the outsider Choir Boy – and in 1954 Aureole won the Coronation Cup, the Hardwicke Stakes and the King George VI and Queen Elizabeth Stakes at Ascot, helping to take the Queen to the top of the owners' list for the first time.

She headed the list again three years later, the same year that she won her first Classic, the Oaks, with Carozza. Since then, two of her most memorable years have been 1974, when Highclere triumphed in the 1,000 Guineas and the French Oaks, and 1977 (the Queen's silver jubilee year) when Dunfermline won the Oaks and the St Leger. The Queen is highly regarded in the racing world for her love of the sport, her ability to 'read' a race in detail, and for her depth of knowledge and understanding of the breeding and training of Thoroughbreds. The stud at Sandringham has been developed into one of the most successful breeding establishments in the country, and has made a major contribution to the British bloodstock industry.

★   ★   ★

There being no opportunity, until the 1970s, to ride in races either on the Flat or over fences, women were restricted to point-to-point racing. The once exception was the Newmarket Town Plate – the only Thoroughbred flat race not run under Jockey Club rules, so the fact that women were not granted Jockey Club licences did not matter. When, on studying the rules laid down by King Charles II in 1665, Miss Betty Tanner realised that no mention was made of women not being allowed to take part, Newmarket suddenly found itself invaded by female jockeys. The first time this happened was in 1923, when five women rode. Two years later Eileen Joel became the first woman to win the Town Plate. There had been a field of seven – two men and five women – so the odds were high for a female victory. Nevertheless Eileen had a convincing win, and second to her was Iris Rickaby, who later became the mother of Lester Piggott. The race, over four miles, is still run each year at Newmarket, where unlicenced jockeys, both men and women, and also those under the permitted age for racing, can compete.

(*above*) Lady Jockeys in Kenya in 1931, and (*below*) Wylye Valley Ladies point-to-point in 1928. Helen Cross leads from Lady Jean Douglas Hamilton, who, in 1921, had won the first ladies race to be held in England.

In 1913, when point-to-pointing established its own charter, the rules did not preclude women from racing against the men, which they frequently did. Most notable among these point-to-point riders in the early 1920s were Miss Wentworth-Reeve, one of the forerunners of a successful group of women riders in East Anglia, and Mrs Mabel Aitken, who at the age of seventy rode her horse Ware Wire into third place in the members' and subscribers' race at the Old Berkshire meeting at Faringdon. She rode side saddle and, according to Michael Williams in *The Continuing Story of Point-to-Point Racing*, 'presented a splendid picture in a green habit and silk hat'. Other winners included Miss V. Selby-Lowndes, who also rode side saddle, and Sylvia Spooner from the West Country, who won over thirty races and was the leading lady rider in England in the 1930s. A week after Sylvia Spooner won at the East Cornwall fixture on 24 April 1929, the Masters of Hounds Association dealt a blow to the women by passing a new rule confining them to 'ladies' races'. The effect was to limit severely their opportunities to compete, since few hunts were prepared to organise ladies' races at the expense of forfeiting one of the other races on their card – usually the men's open. Women were not permitted to compete against men again until 1967.

The first ladies' race was held at the South and West Wilts fixture at Motcombe near Shaftesbury, in 1921. Apparently the Master of the South and West Wilts, Lord Stalbridge, rode behind the contestants in case any of them needed assistance, but it seems that he had considerable trouble keeping up with them. The race was won, from a field of twelve, by Lady Jean Douglas Hamilton (an aunt of Anneli Drummond-Hay, who later became well known both in the eventing and show jumping world), who rode her horse Cavalier II side saddle, and 'went like the wind'.

Women in Ireland did not suffer the same restrictions as the English point-to-point riders, and Mrs Masters, joint Master of the Tipperary, rode over 100 winners during the late '20s and early '30s. Two of the most famous riders in England at this time were Irishwomen – Mrs Evadne Belle, whose husband Isaac Bell was Master of the South and West Wilts for nine years, and their daughter Diana, who was leading lady rider of the season three times between 1933 and 1939.

Between 1949 and 1963 the two outstanding women in point-to-pointing were Pat Rushton (later Mrs John Tollit) and Ida Croxon. They were great rivals, competing in sixty races against each other and finishing either first or second in thirty-one of them. The final score was twenty wins to Pat Rushton, nine to Ida Croxon and two dead-heats. In her time Ida Croxon rode forty-two winners for twenty-two different owners, and Pat Rushton set a new record of 171 winners – a number later surpassed by Mrs Josephine Sheppard who had won no less than 172 races by the start of the 1988 season, making her the most successful lady point-to-point rider of all time. Josephine Sheppard, who is now forty-five, has headed the ladies' championship table five times, in 1969 and from 1974 to 1977. Competitive by nature, she began show jumping 14.2hh ponies as a child, with her brother David Turner (who has ridden more point-to-point winners than any

(*above*) Pat Tollit on Uncle Coke
winning a race at the Worcestershire
Hunt point-to-point in 1965, and
(*below*) Josie Sheppard, the most
successful lady point-to-point rider,
winning the Ladies Open at the
Mid-Surrey Farmers Hunt meeting
in 1974.

Sheilagh French, winner of over 100 point-to-points, riding in the Hertfordshire Ladies Race in 1966.

other person), and had her first chance to race at the age of nineteen, when she won over the Moulton course near Newmarket on a horse called The Babe II. Five years later she won her first Leading Lady title by the narrowest of margins, clinching victory on the last day of the season at the Tiverton Staghounds' meeting.

Two other prolific winners, who at the start of the 1988 season both had a total of 117 wins to their name, are Jenny Pidgeon and Mrs Sheilagh French. Mrs French began her point-to-point career in 1948 when, as Sheilagh Desborough, she had her first ride on a horse called Rare Commotion at the Romney Marsh. Michael Williams takes up the story: 'She had borrowed a 30lb saddle for the occasion and before the race she downed a couple of large whiskies, which possibly explains the fact that when she was hoisted up on the horse she went straight over the other side. Put up again, she started off last, and was still last when she got to the second fence and came upon a horse that had refused. Her horse tried to do the same. So she gave him a kick and he jumped the obstacle from a standstill and shot her over his head.'

The late Sue Horton winning the Ladies Open race at the Exmoor Hunt point-to-point in 1968.

In 1960 the late Sue Horton (née Aston), one of the most talented race riders of her time, won her first point-to-point at the age of fourteen. Two years later the National Hunt Committee saw fit to forbid girls under eighteen from riding in point-to-points, so Sue went to France where she gained valuable experience riding on the Flat for professional trainers, winning numerous races against top-class opposition. Michael Williams wrote that Sue Horton's greatest ambition was to ride in a ladies' hunter chase in England. 'But as the very idea of such a race is enough to give the Jockey Club a heart attack, it seems she will have some time to wait.' Michael Williams' book was published in 1970: six years later, as a direct result of the Sex Discrimination Act, the first female jump jockeys found their way onto the racecourse. By then the Jockey Club had already granted women licences to race on the flat.

★　　　★　　　★

Patricia Cooksey, winner of more than 1,200 races
the USA. She rides at the Turfway Park Racetrack
Kentucky.

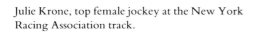

Julie Krone, top female jockey at the New York
Racing Association track.

The pressures on the Jockey Club to allow women to flat race had been considerable. Female jockeys were already competing successfully in other countries, particularly in America, where women had begun riding at recognised Thoroughbred meetings in 1969, following litigation to prevent male jockeys boycotting races in which females were scheduled to ride. Since the Jockey Club accepted foreign jockeys' licences, it could have found itself in the embarrassing position of having to accept the licence of a female jockey wanting to race in England. The Jockey Club was also well aware that there were a growing number of women working in racing stables who had no opportunity to ride in a race because the nature of their work deemed them to be 'professionals'.

What eventually spurred the Jockey Club to take the plunge, however, was some forceful campaigning on behalf of women who wanted to race over jumps. In 1971 Judy Goodhew, wife of permit-holder Charles Goodhew, unwittingly brought the whole question of female jump jockeys into the full glare of publicity by applying for an amateur's licence in her own name. Her application had been prompted by her disgust at the standard of riding of some of the jockeys employed to race their horses. She thought she could do a better job herself. Not surprisingly the Jockey Club turned her down, pointing out that it 'does not grant women licences to ride'. A journalist on the *Sporting Life* had spotted the application and wrote a piece about it, and the press took it up from there. Although the resultant publicity did not have the desired effect as far as would–be female jump jockeys were concerned, it did help to persuade the Jockey Club that the time had come to introduce some ladies' races on the Flat. The following year, on 6 May at Kempton Park, the first of these races took place.

Both Judy Goodhew and Sue Aston were among the twenty-one runners who lined up for the 1 mile 1 furlong Goya Stakes. The race was won by an outsider, Scorched Earth, ridden by Meriel Tufnell, who came in $2\frac{1}{2}$ lengths ahead of Jennifer Barons on Greater. In third place was Sally Hall on Harvest Spider, and Sue Aston came fourth on Straightshooter. 'A Revolution or Nine Days' Wonder?' was the headline of Audax's report in the following week's *Horse and Hound*. 'No doubt,' he wrote, 'the ladies enjoyed it – especially Miss Tufnell, whose victory was the result of much hard work and who, even if she really did have her eyes shut most of the time, continued to ride a tactically flawless race. But all the perfectly understandable satisfaction caused by this successful start does not – or anyway should not – hide the question, where do we go from here? Because the one copper-bottomed certainty is that the glamour, newsworthiness and novelty of last week's contest will, other things being equal, wear off quicker than yesterday's make-up.'

Audax's argument was that the twelve ladies' races scheduled for that season were nothing like enough to produce a reasonable standard of jockeyship among the women, and that unless the standard was good, punters would find the races exceedingly dull to watch. He advocated joint races for women and amateur male jockeys so that there would be plenty of opportunities for all. Four years later, as a result of the Sex Discrimination Act, the problem resolved itself, though it almost went very badly against the female jockeys.

Meriel Tufnell may have been an outsider in the Kempton Park race, but she followed up a victory there with two more, one at Folkestone and one at Newbury, which were enough to make her the first female flat champion. Not long after the historic race at Kempton Park, the Lady Jockey's Association was formed with Meriel Tufnell as its chairman (its present chairman is Mrs Diana Williams). Its aims were based on those of the Jockeys' Association: to maintain the highest standards of honour, integrity and courtesy among lady jockeys and to support and protect their status and interests generally; to promote and afford to members of the Association facilities for mutual consideration, assistance, co-operation, negotiation and information in all matters concerning lady jockeys; to support the best interests of horse racing in every way possible.

The Association's honorary secretary was Dorothy Laird, who, at the time of the LJA's formation, was working at the Racing Information Bureau in Portman Square. When the Jockey Club had first announced its intention to hold an 'experimental six races for ladies' Dorothy Laird had to deal with the enquiries. 'Everyone thought it would be an absolute flop. But we had masses of girls ringing up, and in the end there were so many enquiries that they had to double the number of races to twelve.' The initial enthusiasm has never faltered, and, apart from a break of two years to write one of her twenty-seven books, Dorothy Laird has been the Association's honorary secretary ever since its formation.

By the time the Sex Discrimination Act was introduced in 1975 the LJA had races on every major racecourse in England. Yet when the Act came into effect the Association was in serious danger of losing all its ladies' races. The Equal Opportunities Board at first insisted that there should be no more 'ladies only' races, so that women would at all times have an equal opportunity to race against men. The trouble was, this so-called equal opportunity was not at all equal, because women had not yet had sufficient time and experience on the racecourse to achieve the standard needed to compete successfully against men. The LJA had to move fast to persuade the Equal Opportunities Board that it would not be against women's interests to hold ladies' races. Aided by the personal intervention of the then Minister for Sport, Denis Howell, the Board eventually relented, and the LJA kept most of its fixtures on the basis that they were club races, and the club had been formed before the Act became law. This did not, however, solve the problem of the stable girls, who, as professionals, could no longer compete in races confined to the LJA. Fortunately, the Jockey Club recognised their plight and gave the girls two years' grace before they had to compete as professionals.

The subsequent ten years have been a struggle, and only a handful of women have worked their way into the full professional ranks, most finding that, once out of apprentices, it is even more difficult to get rides. It has been a Catch 22 situation: stable girls are offered few opportunities to race ride, so they do not gain experience and cannot prove themselves to be good jockeys, consequently they are not asked to ride very often. Even when such

Kim Tinkler, the most successful woman Flat jockey.

opportunities do arise they are unlikely to be offered a horse that has more than an outside chance of winning. The prejudices are slowly being swept aside, and many trainers and male jockeys firmly believe that the women can do just as well as the men. Pat Eddery, Champion jockey in 1987, who knows what it feels like to be beaten in a race by a woman, is quoted in a newspaper report as saying: 'They could be as good as us eventually. They're getting better all the time. All they need is more and more experience.'

It was Kim Tinkler, top professional lady jockey of 1986 and 1987, who pipped Pat Eddery to the post twice at the same meeting in August 1987. During that season, which was her first year out of apprentices, Kim rode twenty-one winners – at least twice as many as any other professional female jockey. With no more opportunities to ride in special apprentice races or to claim the weight allowances, the post-apprenticeship season was expected to be a difficult one, but Kim was given a staggering 227 rides, mostly on horses trained by her husband Nigel and owned by the Full Circle Thoroughbred syndicate, an organisation run by her father-in-law, Colin Tinkler. If her connections make it sound easy for Kim to get rides, they disguise an exceptional talent and the result of ten years' hard-earned experience. Members of the syndicate would not ask her to ride their horses if they did not think she was the best person for the job. 'You can go out of fashion so quickly in this game. If you have a lean time, people soon forget about you and ask someone else to ride their horses.' That is one reason why Kim has no intention of increasing the size of her family in the immediate future. She has one daughter, Amy, who was born in 1984. A fortnight after her birth Kim was riding out again, and within two months she was back on a racecourse.

As a young girl Kim had been 'pony mad', and took riding lessons near her Doncaster home, but with little money to spare, the best way to get rides was to go out with the horses from the local racing stables. Kim soon found herself spending most of her evenings and weekends at the stables, and once she had left school took a full time job there. The Sex Discrimination Act had already wreaked havoc on the racing world by then, so when sixteen-year-old Kim rode in her first race she was forced straight into the professional ranks. It took another six years for her to score her first victory. 'At times it was very frustrating. I knew I wasn't riding badly, I just wasn't getting the opportunity to race good horses. It is very difficult for apprentices, men as well as women, to prove themselves if they are not given a chance, and a lot of them lose heart.' Kim changed jobs frequently in those early days to find a yard where there were good horses, so that she would have a better chance of winning. That is how she came to work for Nigel Tinkler, who is now her husband.

After her first win – at Edinburgh on a horse called Wow Wow Wow – Kim's luck began to change. The following season (1986) she had eighteen winners and became the champion Northern apprentice as well as the leading lady jockey. The 1987 season was even better, despite being the only woman in flat racing with a full professional licence. The other forty professional female jockeys were all apprentices (under twenty-five years of age). It is difficult enough for them to get rides, but even tougher for a full professional. 'Things are changing and improving for the female jockeys, but so slowly,' says Kim Tinkler, who has clearly been one of the women hastening those changes.

★   ★   ★

When the Lady Jockey's Association was formed in 1972, included among its honorary members were two people – Florence Nagle and Norah Wilmot – who had been responsible for paving the way for women to hold trainers' licences. Norah Wilmot was the daughter of Sir Robert Wilmot, a successful trainer at Binfield Grove, in Berkshire. She had worked at the stables all her life, riding out and helping to run the yard, and by 1930 was in complete charge, so when her father died a year later she was the obvious successor. Indeed, before his death Sir Robert had written to the Jockey Club to ask for his daughter to be allowed to take over his licence to train, saying that this would make him 'a very happy old man'. But the Jockey Club would not countenance the idea, and Norah Wilmot had to wait another thirty-five years before she could be officially recognised as a trainer. In the meantime Miss Wilmot solved the problem by applying for a licence in the name of her head lad, T. Martin, and within two weeks had produced her first winner at Lewes racecourse. The horse, Bunch, had been bred by Sir Robert and was owned by Percy Johnson, for whom Norah trained many more winners, her best record being nineteen in one season. Other patrons included Lady Yule, Mrs Yeomans, Captain Tyrwhitte-Drake, Baroness Burton, the Queen Mother and HM The Queen. Miss Wilmot also developed a reputation for curing sick and injured horses, and saved the Queen Mother's famous steeplechaser, Devon Loch, after he had broken down in the Mildmay Memorial Chase at Sandown in 1957.

Following Norah Wilmot's example, Florence Nagle was another 'trainer' who had to hold a licence in the name of her head lad. But Mrs Nagle was not content with the Jockey Club's excuses for refusing to issue licences to women – that it would not be in the best interests of racing, and that there was more likely to be a security problem in stables run by women. She decided to sue Sir Randle Fielden and Lord Allendale, as representatives of the Jockey Club, for the right to hold a trainer's licence. Her case went before the High Court in February 1966, where the decision went in her favour. The following August a notice appeared in the Racing Calendar to the effect that Mrs Florence Nagle and Miss Norah Wilmot had been granted licences under Rule 102 of the Rules of Racing for 1966. On the day she received her licence Miss Wilmot won at Brighton, thus becoming the first licenced woman trainer to bring home a winner. Mrs Florence Nagle, who was born in 1894, has remained a staunch supporter of women in racing. Since 1986 she has provided a cup and put up the money for a race at Kempton for female apprentice jockeys.

★   ★   ★

The implications of the 1975 Sex Discrimination Act had put the Jockey Club in a quandary: would it be safe to allow women to race over jumps; how could they be protected? At one time it looked as if the Jockey Club might try to wriggle out of any commitment to licence women jump jockeys by reasoning that they were at a disadvantage because they lacked the same physical strength as men. But women had already shown themselves equal to men in point-to-pointing and three-day eventing, so there seemed to be little choice in the matter. Within three weeks of the introduction of the Sex Discrimination Act the Jockey Club announced that women could apply for amateur and professional licences for National Hunt racing.

A week later six women – Sue Horton, Muriel Naughton, Jane and Diana Thorne, Sheilagh French and Marie Tinkler – presented themselves to the licencing stewards at

Norah Wilmot who, between
1931 and 1966 (before the Jockey
Club permitted women to hold
trainers' licences), successfully
trained racehorses holding a
licence in the name of her head
lad.

Florence Nagle, in February
1966, when her case against
members of the Jockey Club for
the right for women to hold
trainers' licences went before the
High Court.

the Jockey Club's office in Portman Square to make their formal applications for National Hunt licences. Five of them obtained their licences without difficulty, although Sheilagh French had to produce a doctor's certificate because she was 'over thirty-five' (she was actually forty-seven). However, Marie Tinkler, a former show jumper and point-to-point rider, was fifty-one at the time, and was turned down following an examination by the Jockey Club's doctor, a decision that caused an uproar in the press. On 30 January 1976, three days after she had collected her permit from the Jockey Club, Meriel Naughton, the 28-year-old wife of Yorkshire trainer Mick Naughton, became the first women to ride in a National Hunt race. The meeting was at Ayr, and Meriel rode her own Ballycasey in the Spittall Hill amateur riders' handicap chase. She finished last but one in a field of eight, but it was a creditable performance on a horse that was not expected to do better.

The youngest of the five women who first gained their NH licences were the Thorne twins, Diana and Jane, who were then aged twenty-one. Both were experienced event and point-to-point riders (Jane finished second at Badminton in 1977 and fourth in the European Championships at Burghley the same year with The Kingmaker), and within weeks they were riding successfully in hunter-chases. In Diana's first race, at Stratford-on-Avon on 7 February, she beat her father John Thorne to become the first woman to win under NH rules. Remarkably, only two weeks later, and also riding in her first NH race, Jane became the second female jump jockey to score a victory. The most successful woman in that first season was Gillian Fortescue Thomas, formerly a professional motor racing driver, whose three wins and three seconds between January and June 1976 gained her the title of first ladies' champion.

★   ★   ★

'At the post the twenty horses were swaying like the sea. Forward . . . No Good! Back again. Forward . . . No Good! Back again.

'The line formed . . . and rebroke. Waves of the sea. Drawing a breath . . . breaking. Velvet, fifth from the rail between a bay and a brown. The Starter had long since finished his instructions. Nothing more was said aloud, but low oaths flew, the cursing and grumbling flashed like a storm. An eye glanced at her with a look of hate. The breaking of movement was too close to movement to be borne. It was like water clinging to the tilted rim of the glass, like the sound of the dreaded explosion after the great shell has fallen. The will to surge forward overlaid by something delicate and terrible and strong, human obedience at bursting point, but not broken. Horses' eyes gleamed openly, men's eyes sat like chips of steel. Rough man, checked in violence, barely master of himself, barely master of his horse. The Piebald ominously quiet, and nothing coming from him . . . up went the tape.' (Enid Bagnold, *National Velvet*, 1935.)

In 1977 – the second season that racing was opened to female jump jockeys – an even more remarkable piece of history was made: Charlotte Brew became the first woman

(*above*) HRH The Princess Royal at Doncaster in 1987. She brought home her first winner on 3 September 1987, when riding her own Cnoc na Cuille in the Droitwich Chase at Worcester. (*below*) Charlotte Brew at the start of the 1977 Grand National.

to ride in the Grand National. Her decision to enter the National, following a successful first attempt at the Aintree course in the Liverpool Foxhunters race in 1976, caused a great deal of controversy. Many people were of the opinion that to have a Grand National jockey who was both inexperienced and a woman was courting disaster, and that Charlotte Brew would be a danger to other horses and jockeys in the field. Others said she would not be strong enough to tackle the huge fences, and she was accused of deliberately seeking publicity – something which she strived to avoid. She met with much hostility from trainers, and even some of her female colleagues failed to support her.

The publicity surrounding her attempt at the Grand National reached such a pitch that the *News of the World* supplied her with two bodyguards when she attended the pre-race press conference. But her confident statement at the conference: 'I will complete the course and I won't finish last', was not, alas, upheld, as she was forced to withdraw when her horse, Barony Fort, refused to jump the final open ditch, just four fences from home. It was not the most satisfactory result for a real-life National Velvet, but it had been a brave attempt: she had kept out of trouble, kept her head, and done as well as she could on a horse that, although reliable, was slow. He was well behind the rest of the field in the closing stages of the race, and just did not have the incentive to jump the last fences. It was the Grand National at which Red Rum scored his record-breaking third victory, and Miss Brew's failure was hardly noticed amid the tumultous reception given to this hero of the Aintree racecourse.

Since that first assault on the Grand National by a woman, Geraldine Rees, a former event rider, has been the only female to complete the course, a feat she achieved in 1982, riding Cheers. The prospect of a female victory in the Aintree Grand National still looks remote, though the Irish Grand National – Ireland's premier Handicap Steeplechase – has already been won by a woman. In 1984 Mrs Ann Ferris stormed to victory on Bentom Boy, a 33 to 1 outsider, who came in twelve lengths clear of the second horse, Sicilian Answer. Ann Ferris's sister, Rosemary Stewart, was third on Dawson Prince in the same race. These two sisters, born Ann and Rosemary Rooney, followed in their father's footsteps (William Rooney rode over 400 point-to-point winners) to be among Ireland's best known jockeys. In 1976 Ann won the national point-to-point championship, and the following year, with seventeen wins, Rosemary followed suit. Women in Ireland were allowed to take part in National Hunt races a year before the British girls, and Rosemary won her first hunter-chase with a horse called Burly Robert at Navan in 1975. By the end of the 1976–77 season both sisters had each won fifteen races under rules (including the Flat).

In England, the female jockey most likely to succeed in riding a Grand National winner is Gee Armytage. In 1987 she established herself as the leading lady of the sport by becoming the first woman to win against professionals at the Cheltenham Festival. Three weeks later she missed her chance to ride the well-fancied National runner, The Ellier, when she was injured in a fall on the first day of Aintree. The Jockey Club doctor, Michael Allen, refused to let her ride. The Ellier finished seventh. In 1988 she had a second opportunity to ride

Geraldine Rees bringing Cheers home in the 1982 Grand National. She is the only woman to have completed the National.

in the National, this time on her Cheltenham winner Gee A. However, the chance of becoming the second woman to complete the Aintree course was lost two fences before Beecher's on the second circuit when her horse stood off too far and jarred Gee Armytage's back so badly that she was forced to pull up. She had been riding a superb race, disputing the lead for much of the way, and, had she been able to continue, would very likely have been placed.

Gee Armytage's exceptional talent stems from a family steeped in the equestrian world. Her father, Roddy, is a successful trainer, and her mother, Sue Whitehead, is a former international show jumper. Sue's own mother (Gee's grandmother) was Mrs 'Pug' Whitehead, who was a familiar figure on the show jumping circuit in the early post-war years. Originally Gee had intended to follow in her mother's footsteps, but after winning a National Hunt race at the age of sixteen (on which occasion she also became the first woman

Gee Armytage on Gee A jumping the Chair in the 1988 Grand National.

to be fined for excessive use of the whip), she soon became hooked by the racing bug. She is undoubtedly one of the bravest jump jockeys in the business, seemingly undeterred by a terrifying incident in 1986 when her mount bolted off the course onto a dual carriageway, and Gee broke both wrists and elbows. At the beginning of 1988 the 22-year-old jockey decided to turn professional. As an amateur, the Jockey Club had restricted her to seventy-five rides against professionals for the 1987/88 season, and 'it was killing me to wait at home and refuse mounts'. For the previous two seasons she had been the leading lady jump jockey.

Since 1976, the first year in which women in England were allowed to ride under National Hunt rules, female jockeys have won 907 races. Ten winners were ridden by women in the first season; ten years later, in the 1986/87 season, women riders claimed a record 165 wins, firmly establishing their presence in National Hunt racing.

CHAPTER SEVEN
A LIFE WITH HORSES

Jenny Pitman – National Hunt trainer

On 9 April 1983 the eight-year-old Corbiere, ridden by Ben de Haan, ran past the finishing post at Aintree just three-quarters of a length ahead of Greasepaint to win the Grand National and make history for Jenny Pitman. On that day she became the first woman to have trained a Grand National winner.

One of seven children, Jenny (born Jenny Harvey) was brought up on a farm in Leicestershire where ponies were a major influence on her early life. Timmy was her first pony, bought at Melton Mowbray Horse Sale for £20, but there were many others that Jenny would 'sort out' for her younger brothers and friends. The ponies were used by the children for the farm jobs – harrowing, ploughing, carrying hay and checking the sheep – and Jenny would ride her pony to school as well as taking part in illicit races against her cousin around the field of a neighbouring farm. Her greatest calamity in those days was when, at the age of nine, she broke her skull. It happened at a local gymkhana; her pony stopped dead in front of a fence and his young jockey went sailing straight on, colliding head-on with one of the poles. Her cap had left her head almost as easily as she had parted company with her pony, with the result that her skull received the full force of the blow. It took several weeks of tests and examinations before doctors realised what was wrong.

Her first race ride came at the age of fourteen (before the ruling by the National Hunt Committee preventing women under eighteen from competing in point-to-points), on a horse called Dan Archer. She did not win, but nonetheless managed to make a profit on the day by securing the £1 bet that she had made with her uncle to finish the race. A confirmed tomboy, but not a great academic, Jenny left school at fifteen and took a job at a local racing stable, Brooksby Grange Yard, where the horses were trained by Chris Taylor. 'I would have loved, during those days, to become a jockey,' she wrote

Jenny Pitman with her 1984 Cheltenham Gold Cup winner, Burrough Hill Lad.

in her autobiography, but girls were not allowed to ride professionally, and Jenny, being a paid stable girl, was banned from riding in amateur flat races and point-to-points. By the time women were given the go-ahead to race over jumps in 1976 Jenny had married, had two children, and separated from her husband, Richard Pitman.

She and Richard had married in 1965, and after a considerable financial struggle they managed to acquire Hinton Parva Stud, a six-acre establishment where Jenny began taking in a few point-to-point horses. Her very first runner, Road Race, won at Tweseldown, setting the seal on a remarkable first season in which she sent out fourteen horses, won nine races and was second twice. In 1975, nine years after Florence Nagle had taken representatives of the Jockey Club to court to win the right for women to hold trainers' licences, Jenny Pitman took out a licence to train under National Hunt Rules. Her first winner under rules was a horse called Bonidon, who won at Southwell in August that year. But as quickly as Jenny's racing career was taking off, her marriage was floundering, and the following summer Hinton Parva was put on the market so that she and Richard could split the proceeds and go their separate ways.

With her share of the money, and a large loan, Jenny bought a dilapidated house in Upper Lambourn, where she continued to train National Hunt horses. But by the end of 1977 she had reached probably the lowest point in her life. Richard had left her for good, she was in serious debt, and, the day before Christmas, she was rushed to hospital with acute appendicitis. The illness was complicated by a deep abscess in her stomach, and she took many months to recover. Earlier that year, however, she had been to look at a two-year-old at Charles Ratcliffe's yard at Bampton – a very special two-year-old as it turned out. Jenny had liked Corbiere immediately, and the following year he came to her yard for training. By then he had grown so massive and was so slow, that Jenny had serious doubts about her initial instincts. 'He was like a big roly-poly pudding, and my honest feeling was: just how slow can a horse be?' Although fitness work and training soon sharpened him up, he was never a fast horse. His great forte, though, was his tremendous stamina, and it was clear from the start that the longer the race and the heavier the going the better it suited him. Here was a perfect Grand National candidate.

Jenny's earlier hopes of a Grand National victory had been dashed when her best jumper, Lord Gulliver, suffered a heart attack on the gallops at home, crashed into a concrete post, and died. It looked as if she might also lose her chance to run Corbiere in the great race when, in preparation for the 1982 Grand National, he struck into himself on the gallops, damaging a tendon. Fortunately it was only a temporary setback, and although he was out of the race for that year, he came back with a vengeance in 1983 to give Jenny the most memorable triumph of her career.

★   ★   ★

Cynthia Haydon – driving

In the world of driving there is one who stands out above all others, whose skills as a whip are unique and whose success in the show ring unrivalled. Cynthia Haydon is the most renowned driver of hackneys in the world. Hers is the art of classical driving; she is a stylist. Her horses are always immaculately turned out, well schooled and moving beautifully, whether in single harness, pairs, tandems, unicorns or four-in-hand. Few have matched her flair and expertise in a field of equestrianism that is dominated by men. Now in her seventies, Mrs Haydon's reign in the hackney world may not be from the driver's

Cynthia Haydon driving a team of four Hackneys at Lowther.

seat for much longer, but, with her husband Frank, she still runs the most successful hackney stud in Britain, and teaches others the rudiments of good driving, 'I think the ability to drive well is a gift. It is the hardest possible job to pass it on. I can teach people a certain amount, but the rest is up to them.'

Apart from her natural talent, much of Mrs Haydon's expertise has been gained through experience. She has handled so many horses, each with its own character. 'I have spent many hours lying in the bath trying to work out how best to tackle a particular problem with a particular horse. You have to use your head as well as your hands.' But good hands are important, and so is sympathetic handling of the horses. 'I would like to see people driving in the classical way. There is no artistry in competitive cross-country driving.' Mrs Haydon did, however, take part in the early combined driving competitions, and with a team of four hackneys competed in the first FEI World Championships, held in 1972 in Munster, Germany. She was the only woman at the Championships, and competed on the British team, with the late Douglas Nicholson and Sir John Miller, which won the gold medal. Following another successful performance in the 1974 World Championships at Frauenfeld, Switzerland, Mrs Haydon decided to call it a day in this demanding sport and to concentrate on showing – she was already fifty-six years old.

Working with hackney horses had become a way of life for Mrs Haydon from the time when, as a small child in York, she would sit between her uncle's knees as he drove one of the quieter horses in his charge. She left her boarding school at sixteen because she was always bottom of the class and 'my father got fed up with paying the fees'. Her father was Robert Black, the leading professional hackney trainer in England at that time, and Cynthia met her husband Frank when two of his horses came to the Black's yard to be trained and produced. It was here, also, that she met Bertram Mills, the man who was to give her such a valuable start to her driving career. Bertram Mills had a team of hackneys in training with Robert Black, and on seeing Cynthia handle them offered to give her some instruction on driving four-in-hand. After just seven lessons she was sent with his team to the Olympia Horse Show. It was 1936, and the arena in those days was far grander and more imposing than it is now, with banks of flowers, elaborate awnings and so on. Cynthia was only eighteen and had never driven in an indoor arena. 'When

A competitor at Ranelagh in 1887.

the great doors opened I was so terrified I dropped all the reins. Fortunately, my boyfriend [Frank] picked them up for me and shoved them back in my hands.'

The Haydons were married in 1939, and by the end of the war Mrs Haydon had had two sons. After serving with the Royal Fusiliers, Frank came back to civilian life expecting to continue his career as a master butcher; he already had a small chain of shops. But after the war there was a growing interest in hackneys, born out of their use as harness horses to offset petrol shortages. The Haydons already had a small, but good, nucleus of hackneys and people began contacting them for advice. It was not long before the hackney business took over from the butcher business, and Frank Haydon's organisational flair and energy found a new direction. The success of the stud in breeding good quality horses and in producing them to the highest standards was then brought to the attention of a wider audience by the brilliant driving and showing skills of Cynthia Haydon. On thirty occasions since 1949 the Supreme Champion Harness Horse at the National Hackney show has been produced and shown by Mrs Haydon, and on twenty-nine occasions she has produced and shown the Supreme Champion Harness Pony. In 1984, in recognition for her services to equestrian sport, Mrs Haydon was awarded the MBE.

In recent years there has been a tremendous growth of interest in hackneys, with the result that the standards in show classes have improved. 'But,' says Mrs Haydon, 'there is a tendency to put too much emphasis on the action and not enough on confirmation. Some exhibitors will go as far as fixing heavy shoes on the horses to make them accentuate the knee action, but that just makes them plod. The extravagant movement of the hackney should be allowed to develop naturally in schooling. They should look as if they are floating.' From her home in Adlestrop, Gloucestershire, Mrs Haydon continues to train and show hackneys, despite the inconvenience of a metal knee, which works well enough on the flat, but is not so good going up and down stairs. She trains the horses individually, teaching them to respond to vocal commands and to recognise their own name, an essential prerequisite if they are to be driven in a team. Many of her horses have been sold abroad, and for twelve years the Haydons competed regularly on the American show circuit driving a team of hackneys for Commodore Chauncey Stillman of New York. Among hackney enthusiasts throughout the world Mrs Haydon's skills have been admired and respected, her sense of humour enjoyed, and her presence in the arena guaranteed to heighten the atmosphere of any show.

★　　★　　★

Pamela Carruthers – course designer

Designing a course at an international show jumping competition is a nerve-racking experience. If you make it too difficult, the class will be over in the first round, and the riders will be upset because their horses have been over-faced; if you make it too easy, the class could go on all night, and show organisers and television crews will be furious. 'My worst time was at Ascot Spring Show when I was designing the Grand Prix course. Television had asked for no more than eight clear rounds from seventy starters. The first six all went clear, and I felt my career was at an end. Fortunately only two more jumped clear after that, so I was saved.'

Much of the groundwork for designing a course can be done at home. Pamela is sent a plan of the arena, and, working to scale, she maps out her ideas for the major class of the day. If, for example, it is a Grand Prix, she takes that as her starting point, ensuring that she designs a course that will produce a good jump off. She then fits in the other classes around the Grand Prix jumps, so that the course builders do not have to put up an entirely different set of fences for every new class. If the materials to be used are already known to Pamela, that part of the planning can also be done in advance, but heights and distances are never finalised until she knows the conditions and the competitors. 'The riders know I won't make traps for them intentionally, but I'm always prepared to listen to their comments on my courses. I do feel that, as a woman, I must always be sure of my facts, and probably be a little better than the man who might be the alternative selection.' Pamela's outstanding success in her career – she was the first woman to become an international course designer, and has recently become the first female Technical Delegate – stems as much from her own experience of jumping at international level, as from a lively imagination, keen observation and a thorough understanding of the ways in which horses will approach and handle the variety of fences that she puts before them.

As a teenager with a passion for horses, Pamela (née Torrie) was determined to maintain her interest in riding when sent by her parents to a finishing school in Paris. It did not take long to be introduced to some of the leading French show jumpers, and she began riding horses belonging to members of France's international team, competing at the Paris Horse Show and other major shows. She also devised a good scheme to raise the money to buy her own horse: writing to both her mother and grandmother to say how cold the weather was and how badly she needed a fur coat, she duly received two cheques. She never bought the coat, instead spending the money on a two-year-old racehorse which came back to England with her and won the 15hh hack class at Olympia. Pamela also rode the mare to fourth place in an international Grand Prix dressage competition. Success in the show ring continued with a cob called Benjamin, but an incident at the first Horse of the Year Show brought her enjoyment of showing to an abrupt end. Benjamin was poisoned, and although she managed to save him, the incident upset Pamela so much that she vowed never to show again. She began jumping with a horse called Galway Boy, competing at international level for two years before turning her attention to course designing. At first she learnt, mostly by trial and error, to build courses at small local shows, later graduating to the Ascot Spring Show, and in 1960 Douglas Bunn asked her to design the courses at the first Hickstead. It was here that Pamela's reputation was to become firmly established; helped by her excellent courses, Hickstead became the most famous show jumping venue in England, and Pamela, in turn, benefited from being connected with such a prestigious site.

Since then Pamela has been in demand at show jumping competitions all over the world, from New York, Washington and Toronto to France, Germany, Denmark, Spain, Holland, Mexico, Peru, Australia and New Zealand. When she went to Iran in 1979 to build courses at two international shows, she caught the last plane to leave Tehran before the

Shah made his hasty departure from the country. On a trip to America, the astronauts Col Roussa and Col Carr, flew her from Lake Placid to Montreal when she had to get back to Hickstead to build the course for the World Championships.

1987 was one of Pamela's best years. Most of her big classes worked well, and on that good note she decided to 'semi retire'. However, the invitation to be Technical Delegate at the 1988 Olympic Games ensured that she would be kept fully occupied. 'It must be everyone's aim to be involved in the Games, and it was particularly satisfying to be invited to Korea which is very much a man's world.' Pamela's expertise has received worldwide acclaim; she has been given two awards for her course designing, one in Britain and one in the USA, and, in recognition of her work the jumping field at Griffith Park, Los Angeles, opened by Prince Phillip, was named after her.

Pamela Carruthers at the European Show Jumping Championships in 1987.

★　　　★　　　★

Claire Tomlinson – polo player

Claire Tomlinson is the world's leading woman polo player. It was largely because of her outstanding success in the sport and her determination to play at the highest level that, in 1978, the Hurlingham Polo Association was persuaded to change the rules to permit women in Britain to take part in high-goal matches. The following year her team, Los Locos, won the Queen's Cup at Windsor Great Park and, for the first time in history of high-goal polo, the Queen received a curtsey, instead of a bow, from the team member who came forward to receive the cup.

Born into a family with a keen interest in polo (her father gave the name of his Hertfordshire home, Woolmers Park, to his team), Claire 'grew up in a spectator's aura of stick-and-ball and cantering hooves in chukka after chukka and match after match.' J. N. P. Watson, in *The Times* goes on to say, 'But if she was reared on the notion that polo was the finest and most challenging game in the world, her parents also impressed on her that it was reserved for men.'

As a child she had excelled in sports and her studies. She took 'A' level exams at Millfield – one of the few schools in Britain to offer polo on its curriculum – and while there she was selected for the British Junior fencing team. At Oxford she read agricultural economics, finding time to compete for a squash blue and a fencing half-blue, before joining the University polo team. Her first match against Cambridge was won by the Oxford team, and Claire was duly awarded her half-blue. 'With an honours degree and a university travelling award she took a job, in her intellectual field, in Buenos Aires. Her brother, John, having succeeded her father as the mainstay of Woolmers Park, asked her to help him find horses. In the process, she not only learnt a lot about the breeding, making and care of polo ponies, but also, in Argentina's main polo centre, improved out of recognition her knowledge of the game.

'The strength of a woman's arm can rarely, if ever, be that of a man's. But, given her games sense and outstanding coordination of limb and eye, it was not difficult for her to make up for that limitation through the acquisition of a fluent style and mastery of the perfectly timed stroke.'

In 1967 she helped to form a team, Los Locos, with friends. One of them was a young cavalry officer, Simon Tomlinson, and the following year he and Claire were married. 'Their polo went from strength to strength; their mutually supporting partnership in Los Locos forward positions soon became a byword, and so did their talent for recruiting the balance of their teams from players who were most closely in harmony with them. Los Locos carried off nearly all the English low-goal trophies, and in 1977 they won the principal medium-goal prize; Cirencester Park's coveted County Cup.'

Claire Tomlinson, the world's top handicap woman polo player.

By 1978 Los Locos was ready for the high-goal scene (tournaments open to teams whose aggregate handicap is between 17–22 goals). 'When the Hurlingham Polo Association reminded them of the rule against women playing in high-goal matches, Claire Tomlinson, who was then handicap three and had played with 25-goal teams in Argentina, wanted to know why Britain should be the only country in the world with such an illogical stricture. The association remained adamant: Mrs Tomlinson and the other leading British woman player, Lavinia Black, organised a petition proposing that either they should be allowed to take part or their handicaps should be reduced below the recognised high-goal standard. The association relented.'

The Tomlinsons live with their three children at Downs Farm in Gloucestershire, where they breed and train their own ponies. For polo players to succeed at the highest levels of this sport they must have first-class ponies that have been well schooled and have a thorough grounding in the game. Through their expertise and knowledge of the sport the Tomlinsons have produced such ponies, enabling them to compete successfully in high-goal polo in Britain for the last ten years. Polo is the fastest team contest in the world; it is also one of the most complex games to learn. Few women have proved themselves equal to men in this tough, unforgiving sport, but Claire Tomlinson has shown that it is possible. Her understanding of the game and her exceptional athletic ability, combined with courage, determination and a will to win, have enabled her to master the sport at its highest levels.

The Grace sisters – Jane, Pippa, Victoria and Katie – champion girls team.

Val Long – long distance rider

It was in response to a letter published in *Horse and Hound* in 1974 that Val Long became involved in her first long distance riding competition. A forty-mile EHPS (Endurance Horse and Pony Society) ride was being organised for the first time in Cwm Fforrest, Crickhowell, near to where Val was working, and she decided to enter. Riding her 14hh New Forest pony Ashdean Ruler (nicknamed Gunner), she won the competition – an encouraging start, and one that was to eventually lead to her gaining a team gold medal in the first ever World Championships in long distance riding, held in 1986.

Born in London in 1948 to a family with no interest in horses (her father is a landscape gardener), Val grew up 'completely pony mad', and at the earliest opportunity took a job with horses. Later she moved to Dorset to work in a riding stable, but her wanderlust nature soon got the better of her; in 1970 she set forth with Gunner on an expedition to Wales, a journey of at least 200 miles including detours to take in Malvern and other places of interest. It would have cost too much to transport her pony by horsebox, so she rode all the way, camping out overnight, and eventually arriving in Tregaron.

While working in Wales, still with ponies, Val was offered the chance to buy a six-month Arab colt from a stud near Lampeter, 'I couldn't afford him, but was allowed to take him on the never-never, paying over the next three years.' The colt's name was Tarim, and eight years later he and Val set a new British record for the 100 mile Summer Solstice ride, completing the course at an average speed of 10.1 mph, after a race for the finishing post with three other competitors. It was their third attempt at the 100 miles, but in the previous two years Tarim had been too immature, both physically and mentally, to cope with the full distance. 'In hindsight,' says Val, 'I wouldn't enter a horse in a 100-mile ride until it was eight years old, but I wasn't experienced enough at the time to realise that.'

In 1986, following her second win in the Summer Solstice, Val sought permission from the British Horse Society to take Tarim to Rome, the venue for the first World Championships, as an individual competitor. 'I hadn't previously been a member of the BHS Long Distance Riding Group, so I was not eligible for selection for the team. But I suddenly realised it would be foolish of me to miss the chance to compete in the World Championships, so I applied to go as a self-financing individual. That was also foolish, because I then had to take out a £2,000 overdraft and borrow a cattle wagon to get there.' The British organisers were only too glad to see Val in Rome. One of their squad had dropped out, and Val soon found herself seconded onto the team. In another neck and neck finish, Val and Tarim galloped into fourth place, helping the British team to win the gold medal. It was a good day for the women: out of the first four individual places three went to females, and the victorious British team was made up entirely of women – Val Long, Carol Tuggey, Pam James and Denise Passant.

In Britain the sport of long distance riding has been dominated by women. In 1987 Britain sent another all-female squad to the European Championships in Germany. The

Val Long and her Arab Stallion Tarim competing in the Golden Horseshoe Ride in 1987.

team finished fourth, Val and Tarim came seventh, and Liz Finney won the individual silver medal. In 1965, when the first Golden Horseshoe Ride was held on Exmoor, the top award went to a woman, and since its inaugural competition in 1975, the 100-mile Summer Solstice ride has always been won by a woman.

★　　　★　　　★

Annette Yarrow – sculptor

Among equestrian artists Annette Yarrow is one of the most exciting sculptors of today. Her work, mostly in bronze, spans the full equestrian sphere, from polo, racing and eventing to what she regards as her greatest project – a life-size Bedouin warrior mounted on an Arab mare, a commision from HM King Hussein of Jordan, which now stands, floodlit at night, in the city of Amman.

It was quite by chance that Annette entered the world of equestrian art. Alighting upon some modelling clay one day at her Renfrewshire home, she attempted to mould it into a small model of the head of her youngest son, David; to her amazement, she found that the result actually looked like him. With no formal training in art, Annette, then aged thirty-four and with a family of four boys, had suddenly discovered that she possessed that rare ability to capture a 'likeness'. She had had a lot to learn, mostly by trial and error, but with encouragement from the foundry in London where her sculptors were cast, she soon began producing good work. Her choice of equestrian subjects stemmed from a background steeped in horses. On the tea estate in southern India where she was brought up horses were very much a way of life, for work and pleasure, and Annette always had ponies to ride. She won her first race at the age of eight on a pony called Peter.

An education at Cheltenham was followed by nursing training in Glasgow before she returned to India. As Matron at a nursing home in Madras she was able to combine her job with her love of race riding, and for three consecutive years was the champion amateur jockey of South India. In 1980 Annette married the photographer John Elliot, and set up home in the New Forest. They now work as a team, John helping Annette with the engineering technicalities of her sculpting, and Annette acting as assistant photographer when John is working, whether at an equestrian event, a sailing regatta or a wedding. Annette's studio, made from an old cart shed, overlooks the paddock where her Arab mare, Halba, who was bought as a model especially for the Bedouin sculpture, runs out. 'I can watch her from the window and learn so much about a horse's movements.' John also takes photographs of Halba to help Annette, but most of the sculpting is done from her imagination. Years of watching and riding horses have given her an instinctive feel for her subjects, and as she works the plasticine by hand the picture that she has in the back of her mind begins to take shape. Not surprisingly, her work is renowned for its sense of freedom and movement.

Annette Yarrow working at her home in Hampshire.

Retaining her professional name, Yarrow, from her previous marriage to Lord Yarrow, Annette was already carrying out commissions for Aspreys of Bond Street when Queen Noor, wife of King Hussein, saw some of her work in the shop. 'I had a phone call from Asprey's asking if I could go to Jordan to do a sculpture of the King's favourite horse,

Baharein. I said I could, on condition that John came with me. At six o'clock the next morning the Queen's secretary rang to say that we were booked on a flight to Jordan at midday! With dogs and horses at home, it was impossible to leave at such short notice, but three days later we were in Amman.'

The sculpture was to be a surprise birthday present for the King, so the initial work had to be completed within two weeks, before the King and Queen returned from a visit in America, but Annette had no idea what sort of sculpture the Queen had in mind or how big it should be. Fortunately, on seeing the plasticine model the Queen was delighted, and immediately dispatched Annette and John back to London to have it cast in bronze. On a subsequent visit to Amman, they took with them a small model of a Bedouin riding a horse, an idea which they hoped might interest King Hussein. When the King saw it, he thought it was splendid, and promptly asked Annette if she could make a life-size sculpture for the centre of the city. Astounded, Annette immediately agreed to do it, although 'the thought of such a huge undertaking made me feel quite weak'. It was a fantastic project, and at times the sheer logistics of creating this vast work of art seemed insuperable, but with the innovative use of material, many hours of painstaking work, and a few anxious moments, the sculpture took shape.

When the finished bronze, weighing over a ton, was finally delivered from the foundry to the Elliot's home, it sat on the drive outside their kitchen window for another year until its site in Amman, outside the new Parliament buildings, was ready to receive it. At last the message came through that John and Annette were to supervise its transport to Jordan and see it put safely in position. 'It was a bit of a nightmare,' relates John. 'I was convinced the bronze would be dropped. Among other problems, I had the greatest difficulty in getting the Jordanian crane driver to understand my English instructions. This was further complicated by a growing crowd of inquisitive passers-by who had stopped to watch the proceedings and began directing the crane driver in Arabic.' Eventually, much to everyone's relief, the majestic bronze was secured on its marble base, ready for the official unveiling by King Hussein.

Annette continues to produce sculptures for Aspreys, as well as carrying out private commissions. Included among her work is a bronze of Princess Anne on her event horse, Doublet, and more recently she has diversified from equestrian subjects to produce a life-size eagle on a globe of the world for the Army Air Corps memorial, and a Badger and Cubs for the British Wildlife Appeal.

NOTES

1 (page 16)   *A History of the English-Speaking Peoples* (Vol. 1) by Winston S. Churchill, Cassell, 1956.

2 (page 24)   *Encyclopaedia Britannica*.

3 (page 24)   *Marie Antoinette* by Desmond Marshall, Constable 1981.

4 (page 24)   *Ladies of the Chase* by Meriel Buxton, The Sportsman's Press, 1987.

5 (page 34)   *Skittles: The Last Victorian Courtesan* by Henry Blyth, Hart-Davis, 1972.

6 (page 40)   *History of the Pytchley and Althrop Hunt 1634–1920* by Guy Paget, 1937.

7 (page 42)   *Ladies of the Chase by Meriel Buxton*, The Sportsman's Press, 1987.

8 (page 49)   *Hoofs in the Distance* by Lida L. Fleitmann (Mrs J. Van S. Bloodgood), D. Van Nostrand, 1953.

9 (page 53)   *Jump for Joy* by Pat Smythe, Cassell, 1954.

10 (page 74)   *The Horse Trials Story* by Lt Col C.E.G. Hope, Pelham Books, 1969.

11 (page 111)   *The Derby* by Michael Wynn Jones, Croom Helm, 1979.

BIBLIOGRAPHY

Alcock, Anne, *They're Off: The story of the first girl jump jockeys*, J. A. Allen, 1978.

Apsley, Lady, *Bridleways Through History*, Hutchinson, 1936.

Bagnold, Enid, *National Velvet*, William Heinemann, 1935.

Bellamy, Joyce, *Hyde Park for Horsemanship*, J. A. Allen, 1975.

Blow, Simon, *Fields Elysian: A Portrait of Hunting Society*, J. M. Dent, 1983.

Blyth, Henry, *Skittles: The Last Victorian Courtesan*, Hart–Davis, 1972.

Buxton, Meriel, *Ladies of the Chase*, The Sportsman's Press, 1987.

Campbell, Judith, *Royal Horses*, New English Library, 1983.

Chenevix Trench, Charles, *A History of Horsemanship*, Longman, 1970.

Churchill, Winston S., *A History of the English-speaking Peoples*, (Vol. 1), Cassell, 1956.

Cleaver, Hylton, *They've Won Their Spurs*, Robert Hale, 1956.

Draper, Judith, *Show Jumping: Records, Facts and Champions*, Guinness Books, 1987.

Encyclopaedia Britannica, The

Fairfax–Blakeborough, J., *The Northern Turf History*, Vol. 3.

Fane, Lady Augusta, *Chit Chat*, Thornton Butterworth, 1926.

Feiling, Keith, *A History of England*, Book Club Associates, 1975.

Fleitmann, Lida L. (Mrs J. Van S. Bloodgood), *Hoofs in the Distance*, D. Van Nostrand, 1953.

    The Saddle of Queens, J. A. Allen, 1959.

Graves, Robert, *The Greek Myths*, Penguin, 1955.

Grimshaw, Anne, *The Horse: A Bibliography of British Books 1851–1976*, The Library Association, 1982.

Hartley Edwards, Elwyn, *Horses: Their Role in the History of Man*, Willow Books, 1987.

Holgate, Virginia, *Ginny, An Autobiography*, Stanley Paul, 1986.

Hope, Lt Col C. E. G., *The Horse Trials Story*, Pelham Books, 1969.

L'Annee Hippique 1987/1988, Henk Bruger.

Macgregor-Morris, Pamela, *Show Jumping: Officers' Hobby into International Sport*, David & Charles, 1975.

Marshall, Desmond, *Marie Antoinette*, Constable, 1981.

Marshall, Rosalind K., *Mary, Queen of Scots*, Crown Copyright, 1986.

Martin, Ann, *The Equestrian Woman*, Paddington Press, 1979.

Mythology, New Larousse Encyclopedia of, Hamlyn, 1959.

O'Donoghue (Nannie Lambert), *Ladies on Horseback*, W. H. Allen, 1889.

Olympic Three-Day Event: Los Angeles '84, Threshold Books, 1984.

Orton, John, *Turf Annals of York and Doncaster*, H. Sotheran, York, 1844.

Owen, Rosamund, *The Art of Side Saddle*, Tremarton Press, 1984.

Paget, Guy, *History of the Pytchley and Althrop Hunt 1634–1920*, 1937.

Pitman, Jenny, *Glorious Uncertainty*, Willow Books, 1984.

Prior-Palmer, Lucinda, *Up, Up and Away*, Pelham Books, 1978.

Ramsden, Caroline, *Ladies in Racing*, Stanley Paul, 1973.

Severs, Malcolm, *Caroline Bradley, A Tribute*, Harrap, 1983.

Shedden, Lady Diana and Lady Apsley, *To Whom the Goddess*, Hutchinson, 1932.

Smith, Alan, and Brian Giles, *The SR Direct Mail Book of Eventing*, Stanley Paul, 1984.

Smythe, Pat, *Jump for Joy*, Cassell, 1954.

    Show Jumping, Cassell, 1967.

Surtees, R. S., *Mr Sponge's Sporting Tour*, Bradbury and Evans, 1953.

    Ask Mama, Bradbury and Evans, 1958.

Trollope, Anthony, *Hunting Sketches*, Chapman & Hall, 1985.

Walker, Stella A., *Long Live the Horse, An Anthology*, Country Life, 1955.

Wallechisky, David, *The Complete Book of the Olympics*, Penguin Books, 1984.

Watson, J. N. P., *The World of Polo, Past and Present*, The Sportsman's Press, 1986.

Whyte-Melville, G. J., *Market Harborough*, Country Life Books, 1984.

Williams, Michael, *The Continuing Story of Point-To-Point Racing*, Pelham Books, 1970.

Willy, Margaret, *Three Women Diarists*, 1964.

Wynn Jones, Michael, *The Derby*, Croom Helm, 1979.

INDEX